# Serendipity

_or_

# Passion?

Building a Successful Business
One Lesson at a Time

# Serendipity

*or*

# Passion?

## Stephanie V. Blackwell

FOUNDER *of* AURORA PRODUCTS, INC.

*Advantage*.

Published by Advantage, Charleston, South Carolina.
Member of Advantage Media Group.

ADVANTAGE is a registered trademark, and the Advantage colophon is a trademark of Advantage Media Group, Inc.

Printed in the United States of America.

10 9 8 7 6 5 4 3 2 1

ISBN: 978-1-64225-342-9
LCCN: 2021922424

Cover design by David Taylor.
Layout design by Mary Hamilton.

This publication is designed to provide accurate and authoritative information in regard to the subject matter covered. It is sold with the understanding that the publisher is not engaged in rendering legal, accounting, or other professional services. If legal advice or other expert assistance is required, the services of a competent professional person should be sought.

*I dedicate this book to all the people and employees I have worked with for the past thirty-plus years, both at Aurora Products and its predecessor, Amalgamated Produce. Many tales in this book would not have happened without your enriching my life and sharing in my passion.*

# CONTENTS

# PREFACE

**S**ometimes I receive calls and solicitations from individuals, universities, women's leadership groups, and other clubs and organizations asking, "Would you be a guest speaker at our organization on your business?" or "How did you start your business, Aurora Products?" The answer to how Aurora was created is not a short one. It goes back to my childhood and the very formation of who I am. It also stems from the many tribulations I experienced in previous endeavors. I have learned that perseverance, luck, and passion are critical factors in starting a successful business.

I am lucky to have lots of passion for what I do and where I am in life—hence the title *Serendipity or Passion?* The answer to the question is *both*. The hardest thing for me in starting a successful business was finding a viable idea that captured my motivation *and* passion. Once I found it, I could not stop myself even if I tried.

This book recounts humorous moments, sad times, great times, stressful situations, and challenging business decisions and strategies. I have tried to write events in sequence, but it is sometimes tricky, and the tale must be contained to a specific topic. If you are lucky enough to start your own business, particularly in the manufacturing or processing of food products, I hope you'll learn some pitfalls to avoid from the lessons revealed in these pages.

My only regret is having started Aurora Products in my mid-forties. I'm having so much fun at sixty-eight years old and have so much more to do. Yet I'm not going to let age keep me back.

# ACKNOWLEDGMENTS

I am thankful for the experiences and knowledge acquired over the years from my family. Entrepreneurs have their ups and downs, and they need to pick themselves up until they succeed. My family helped me do just that.

I also acknowledge my pastor, David Rowe, of Greenfield Hill Congregational Church, who encouraged me to publish this book by writing the following message:

> *May I strongly encourage you to do the writing you are thinking about?... It can be so important on many levels... You will love doing it, your family will be blessed by reading it... When I first moved here, Gene Moore was still alive... Did you know him and Edie?... Gene really lived the classic post-depression, post-war, American dream type of life—successful businessman in manufacturing in Bridgeport's heyday, a true gentleman, a person of faith... Anyway, one day he gave me his self-published autobiography to read, and what*

*insights and lessons there were in there for anyone who cared to find them!!... Those who have lives with such experiences can share them in a way that extends the legacy.*

# GROWTH OF AN ENTREPRENEUR

## *In The Beginning*

*See, when you drive home today, you've got a big windshield on the front of your car. And you've got a little bitty rearview mirror. And the reason the windshield is so large and the rearview mirror is so small is because what's happened in your past is not near as important as what's in your future.*

—JOEL OSTEEN

"Stephanie, I'm waiting for the contractor to get back to me on his quote for the new addition," says Scott as Colleen leaves my office after discussing an issue about employee benefits.

Lyn barges in, interrupting my conversation with Scott, asking if I can approve some invoices and sign off on the automated clearinghouse (ACH) payments.

"I was here first!" blurts out Chris, who has been patiently waiting for my answer to a question concerning commissions to a broker.

I'm waiting for a ten thirty conference call with a buyer and am anxious for everybody to leave my office. Such a hectic day, yet I love every minute of it.

Aurora Products is my baby. It is a manufacturer of all-natural snacks and was built twenty-two years ago by passion, hard work, and serendipitous timing. It has grown from only four employees to over two hundred by processing and packaging healthy nuts, dried fruits, granolas, and other items for supermarket chains nationwide. I am proud not only of what *I* have accomplished but also of all the teamwork it took to get us where we are. Aurora is like a beehive without the stingers. Everyone has a job to do and cooperates to get things done in a coordinated, though hectic, fashion.

I sit here at my desk, looking at all the activities around me while reminiscing on my life. I love where I am now at sixty-eight years old and am excited to share my story. It was a journey that took years to unfold. I experienced several failed business endeavors, had four children, married three men, and finally ended up with a successful, wonderful business. Maybe by reading this book, your journey can go a bit more smoothly. Let's begin, as they say, at the beginning.

\* \* \*

I was born in August 1952 in Kingston, New York, and named Stephanie Lynn Vogel. I suspect my parents wanted a little boy after having my older sister, but they never said anything. My father was the last Vogel in the family and looked forward to having a namesake.

My parents brought home all seven pounds, ten ounces of me to Stone Ridge, New York, nestled in the Shawangunk Mountains and about nine miles from Kingston. Stone Ridge was a rural farm town with several old stone homes from the early 1700s to late 1800s and farms used for raising cattle and growing crops. My grandfather built the elementary school in 1951 and embedded my older sister's white booties in the cornerstone. Most people in Stone Ridge were lower-middle class and were either farmers or workers in Kingston. Our house was an old, white farmhouse built in the mid-1800s with low ceilings and a green tin roof.

One of my father's friends, Mr. Felson, had to lean down when he entered the living room to avoid the beam. He would forget to duck now and then, and I'd hear him cursing "damn!" as he rubbed his forehead. He was six foot five. My dad was six feet tall and could barely walk under the beam. In the backyard there was an outhouse and a chicken coop big enough to hold our twelve Rhode Island Reds. There was also a storage room in the cellar of an outside storage shed that my father converted to a bomb shelter during the Cuban missile crisis. "Someday we may need this shelter, and you'll all be glad we have it," my father would tell us. We never used it.

As a chore my sister and I were often assigned the task of weeding the gravel driveway, which we hated. Often our hands would wrap around a rotting apricot that had fallen off the tree in the middle of the circular drive. I loved the blossoms of the apricot tree, and the fruit was sweet. The rotting fruit in the gravel was another story.

I would sometimes run across the street to Lowes, the local gas station/ministore, to buy my favorite candy, Fireballs, for one cent each, or a Coke from the soda machine for ten cents. Mr. Lee would be sitting there in a chair, reading a newspaper and smoking a cigarette. He was a thin man who had a few black front teeth and smelled like cows. To me he looked old, but in retrospect I think he was much younger than my initial estimate as a seven-year-old—maybe only in his thirties. As a farmer whose property lay down the road, he would work early in the morning and have a long break before heading back in the evening to milk the cows. So Mr. Lee would go to the gas station and visit Mr. Lowe every day to catch up on things.

Stone Ridge consisted of one quaint library built during the Revolutionary War, Lowes, and a post office no larger than twelve by fifteen feet. To go supermarket shopping to stock your kitchen, you needed to drive into Kingston. For incidentals such as a quart of milk or loaf of bread, you could try Lowes. A local bank, where I religiously put twenty-five cents a week into my Christmas savings account, was eventually built across the street from our house. Usually I had put all twelve dollars and fifty cents in my account by August, whereas my siblings tended not to finish by the time Christmas came rolling around. No restaurants or quick food stops were available in Stone Ridge. You had to drive into Kingston or up the road about six miles to a small pizza shop. The pizza restaurant was hard to find along the road and looked isolated among the scattered houses and farms.

\* \* \*

My first introduction to the business world started with tag sales at seven years old. My sister and I would set up our goods on a wall in the side yard—old dolls we didn't want, my mom's retired evening heels rescued from her wastebasket, old books—and hope for customers to come by. Unfortunately we lived in the country until I was twelve, and the only customers were our little brother, an occasional visiting relative, and Mrs. Boehm, our sixty-five-year-old German babysitter. She came every Saturday night for our parents' date night.

Mrs. Boehm was a stocky woman with long gray hair that she braided and put in a circular bun behind her head. She loved to watch *The Perry Como Show* on Saturday evenings, followed by *Bonanza*, my favorite show. I was in love with one of the series stars, Hoss, the heavyset middle brother. He was like a big teddy bear with a kind heart. She was in love with Little Joe, the roguish youngest brother, who I admit was cute. Mrs. Boehm rarely bought anything at our tag sales, and our little brother showed no interest, nor did he ever have any money left from his allowance of five cents. Tag sales were the first of many business failures to come.

Our next venture was a cotton candy stand we set up on Route 209. That was the main street, and at least one car came rambling down the road every other minute. We used the cotton candy maker we got for Christmas to make the pink, fluffy snack. We were sure it would fly like hotcakes. Our home was on Route 209, and my mother let us set up a table on the front lawn steps to the street. We made a big sign, "Cotton candy with free tomatoes." Since my parents had a large garden, they had a surplus of tomatoes and let us have some. We thought we would throw in the tomatoes to help our mom unload her vast crop.

"Come get your cotton candy with some free tomatoes!" It was amazing how many people stopped at our stand. Some got their free tomatoes but forgot to take their cotton candy. It never dawned on me that they only wanted the tomatoes until the following year, when we tried selling lemonade. A couple of cars stopped by, asking us if there were any "bonus tomatoes," and they seemed disappointed when we said no.

My third and last business endeavor as a minor started during my senior year in high school after moving to Kingston. I decided to sell Avon cosmetics. I received a blue kit filled with samples and order forms. Unfortunately I did not understand cosmetics and knew very little about skin foundation, eye creams, cheek powders, or lipstick textures. Therefore, there wasn't much need for order forms. My parents were strict and wouldn't allow my sister or me to wear makeup until we were seniors in high school. Being more of a girly girl than me, my sister loved makeup and would often put it on her face, only to wipe it off after getting off the school bus. Sometimes my father would find her stash of makeup and confiscate it. As for me I only wore mascara and wasn't interested in anything else.

I sold a bit of makeup to my female relatives. Then when I ran out of relatives, I decided to reach out to the neighborhood. It was only after stopping at a few households that I began to realize that being a salesgirl for a product you were not passionate about was difficult. I dreaded going door to door, asking the woman of the house if she wanted to purchase makeup. What if she asked me questions that I couldn't answer? The final straw landed when I rang the doorbell of an unknown neighbor.

> **If you don't have passion, or at least a modicum of interest in your product, success is much harder to obtain.**

An elderly lady came to the door, and I quickly blurted out, "You don't want to buy any Avon products, do you?" I wanted to get it over with and go home.

She sadly replied, "No, dear."

That was the end of my Avon career and a lesson that followed me for years to come. Being a good salesperson, at least for me, requires commitment, knowledge, and most of all, passion for what you are selling. If you don't have passion, or at least a modicum of interest in your product, success is much harder to obtain.

* * *

I was very much a saver as a child. It seems some children are just born this way since my older sister and I didn't share this trait. Sometimes I reminisce about the time I buried a coin under some bushes in front of my home to save for the future. I put a treasured dime from my twenty-five-cent allowance into one of those little pirate chests you got from the dentists to put your tooth in for the tooth fairy. It was barely large enough to hold a dime, but I managed to stuff it in. Did other kids do this? There are days when I feel like going back to that bush to find the dime, but I don't think the new homeowners would appreciate a strange sixty-eight-year-old woman digging up their front yard. Perhaps I could tell them I was looking for a treasure chest filled with money. They wouldn't need to know all the details.

In the 1950s and '60s, entering the business world as a woman was more challenging than it is today. I don't remember any woman business acquaintances of my parents, except my mother's hairdresser and cleaning lady. All her friends were stay-at-home mothers and belonged to the Junior League, Garden Club, or PTA. Men were the breadwinners and expected to use their skills to take care of the family. If a woman had to work—as a secretary, teacher, or nurse—it was not out of choice but necessity.

I often heard Mom and Dad discuss a couple they knew. A typical conversation would be "Oh, they're such a nice couple. I like Bob. He did such a great job in finishing his house. And Judy—well, she is a bright woman in her own right."

I would ask them, "What do you mean by that?" I didn't like the implications. I felt it was insulting to refer to the work on the house as a credit to the man while mentioning the woman's intelligence as if it was a footnote.

One day my father decided to cook dinner. When he proudly announced his intentions, my siblings and I laughed at him, stating that cooking was Mom's job. He informed us in a professor-like manner that the best cooks in the world were men. After all how many woman chefs did you see? He told us, "Children, if you do your research, you will find that men are as good as, if not better than, women in many things you assume to be women's work. More men are chefs and tailors than women. A female can become a seamstress, but the real talent lies in tailoring, where clothes are fitted to suit."

My mother agreed, which to this day I find confusing. I felt deflated and somewhat insecure, thinking, *Well, where is it that women excel besides child-rearing and teaching?* Not until later did I realize that women were often locked out of good positions as chefs or tailors, because it was still a man's world in the '60s.

\* \* \*

Mom and Dad encouraged their two older daughters (which included me) to go to college to become teachers or to follow careers that would augment their husbands' income. That way if there were a divorce, we would be prepared to support ourselves with a field to fall back on.

I was raised in a traditional family where the man brought home the bacon and the woman cooked it. I did not know what business was. If there were any ownership or management transition discussions regarding the family business my father co-owned, they did not include my older sister, Valerie, or me. My brother was the natural successor until he showed no interest in becoming heir to the throne. To their credit, as my parents aged, they adapted to more contemporary social and economic norms.

My younger sister, Bianca, was half a generation younger than I was and benefited from the changing times and increased opportunities for women. As Dad got older, he had nobody to succeed him in running the business since my brother had other plans and the two older daughters had already established their lives. My younger sister was smart, an engineer from Rensselaer Polytechnic Institute, and married a classmate from the same school. She and her husband bought Ertel Engineering Corporation, the filtration company my dad owned. They are now the third generation to run the business and have done a fantastic job in its continued growth. My grandfather Fred Ertel started the company in 1932 and made filters from asbestos and wood pulp used in the production of penicillin. Today the filters are manufactured from wood pulp, without asbestos, and are used in making the vaccine for COVID-19.

\* \* \*

My father, George, bought his father-in-law's business in 1964 with my Uncle Jack. Jack St. John was a wealthy man and one of the leaders of Kingston. His looks and smooth personality reminded me of Ronald Reagan, who could schmooze anyone with his charm. I admired Uncle Jack. He was a successful attorney who had held the district attorney's office for Ulster County at age twenty-eight. Uncle Jack had no desire to run the company with my father but preferred to take on the role of silent partner and advisor.

My family left Stone Ridge and relocated to Kingston that same year, making it easier for my father to be close to his business and for his children to be closer to friends and activities. We moved into an old Victorian house that is listed on Wikipedia as a historical home. It was built in the 1800s and had old, velvet-covered wallpaper, chandeliers with glass baubles, and servants' quarters on the third floor with a separate bathroom. There was a button under the carpet in the main dining room that the head of the household would step on to call the cook into the dining room. Of course, my parents' only servants were their kids, who did odd chores around the house.

The garage was set back about a hundred yards from the house to accommodate the horses and carriages used for transportation in the 1800s. The top of the garage was originally used to store hay. The home and garage—or barn—have been modernized but still have some features from 150 years ago. My teenage years were spent in this house, growing up with my older sister, Valerie; my younger brother, George; and the new baby, Bianca.

I hated it when my parents would lump my sister and me into the category of "the girls". Mom and Dad felt that girls needed to be protected, whereas the son should experience life more freely. It was frustrating for me and my first introduction to the Great Double Standard. Mom would let one of the girls clean the oven to make some extra money. I was ambitious about adding to my piggy bank; therefore, I did most of the oven cleaning. I worked for hours scrubbing away on the oven and ended up with raw, red hands and broken nails. I can still remember the noxious fumes from the Easy-Off oven-cleaning spray, which did not live up to its name. This was in the days before my parents bought a self-cleaning oven. What a wonderful invention!

When I finished the job, Mom would give me three dollars. My brother, on the other hand, would use the motorized snowblower to clear the snow, which took about forty-five minutes. He would be paid six dollars. I complained about the inequity but got nowhere. Dad would chuckle and tell me that I was acting like a bra burner.

"Bra burning" was a derogatory term used in the '60s to refer to women rebelling against sexual discrimination. It was based on the act of a few protesters who supposedly once threw their bras into a bonfire to make a symbolic statement. Maybe Dad's use of the term was the beginning of my awareness of the huge inequities in respect, expectations, and pay between men and women, and I wouldn't say I liked it. When my grandfather died, he left some money for my brother to go to college. It wasn't much, but the expectations for a male over a female hurt.

I rarely discussed these inequities but always felt their undercurrent. However, to use a favorite quote from Martin Luther King Jr., "Our lives begin to end the day we become silent about things that matter." So periodically I would not be silent. I remember telling my parents and peers that I would have preferred to be born a male, although I was secure in my sexuality as a female. I understood the privileges of being a male and identified more with that role. I played with dolls and imagined myself as a wife and mother, yet I also wanted to work outside the home and have the responsibilities and perks of a man. I didn't like the glass ceiling I came up against as a child and as a developing young woman. I also resented being lumped into "the girls," since my sister and I were very different and followed different paths.

\* \* \*

During my senior year at Kingston High School, I applied to several colleges for my bachelor's degree. I wasn't interested in further education, especially if it entailed sitting in a classroom, yet I understood that a degree was necessary if I wanted to get ahead in the world. I had a difficult time sitting still in class. Today I might well have been diagnosed with attention deficit disorder. I dreaded parent-teacher conferences, always fearful of getting into trouble from the teachers' reports.

I remember the day Kennedy died. I was in the sixth grade, and my parents had a parent-teacher meeting that evening. Being too young to understand the gravity of the assassination, I was grateful to Kennedy for allowing the conference to be canceled, even if it meant he had to die that day. Had the meeting not been canceled, my parents would have come home, chastising me about my many reported episodes of not paying attention in class. I was one of those kids who routinely came home from school with chalk marks on their chest from the teacher throwing erasers at them to get their attention. I just could not keep my focus on the subject for more than five minutes. I tried in vain, but the bird outside the window or the fly on the wall would always grab my attention. The worst part was at the end of the day, when I had no idea what homework was assigned. I was always grateful when a teacher put the assignments on the board. My grades, while not excellent, were always good enough to put my name on the honor roll though. So my attention issue went unnoticed, and I was thought of as just lazy or a daydreamer.

\* \* \*

When choosing a college, I decided to attend Wells. At the time, it was an all-women's school in a rural New York town on Cayuga Lake. It had a small campus yet plenty of land and beautiful brick buildings covered with ivy. With fewer than five hundred students, there was plenty of space for one to sit under a tree to muse or sprawl in the grass. Or one could take a walk into the small town, which consisted of an old hotel, a dress shop, and a small grocery store. This was fifty years ago. I don't know much about the school today except that it has turned coed, which is good. I chose biology and chemistry as a double major. The only business course I took was Economics 101.

During summer breaks from college, my parents encouraged all their children to work. One year I was a chambermaid at a Howard Johnson's motel and had to clean ten rooms in about six hours. I was usually the slowest of the eight chambermaids, and they shot me annoyed glances when they had to stay to help me finish up. I tend to be a perfectionist and could not whisk through a room without ensuring all its corners were clean. It is not uncommon for people to accuse me of having obsessive-compulsive disorder. HoJo's was probably the most challenging job I ever had, with the least amount of gratification.

I spent the following three summers interning as a medical lab assistant. As a science major in college, I was hired along with other young students pursuing an education in either medical science or biochemistry. These were memorable years for me. The first year, I worked in the pathology and cytology departments. These departments studied tissues and cells biopsied from patients and sent samples to the lab. In pathology most Pap smears were examined by the staff and reviewed by the pathologist.

I was also asked to assist the pathologist in performing autopsies, a unique experience. I saw my first naked man on the autopsy table and wondered what the fuss was all about—what I saw was quite unimpressive. Performing autopsies didn't bother me since the victim had already passed away. Going into the hospital and dealing with *live* patients was substantially more challenging. Sometimes I would assist the pathologist in obtaining a bone marrow sample from the sternum of some unlucky patient. Most men moaned at the big needle as it suctioned up the marrow. Women tended to be more stoic. Seeing patients in pain can be difficult and emotionally draining to watch. I knew I could never be a doctor.

I spent the second and third summers in other departments, dealing with culture counts, some additional cytology, and pregnancy tests. Until this time pregnancy had been determined by injecting a woman's urine into a female rabbit. When I started working for the labs in the early 1970s, new tests were coming out that did not use rabbits. A woman could pee on a stick. I was involved in assessing the accuracy of these tests versus the older technique. Today younger people have no idea what it means when someone refers to the rabbit having died in a conversation about being pregnant. When you hear that the rabbit died, you can be excited (or not) at the prospect of having a baby within the next few months. Yet I still feel sorry for the poor, nonexistent rabbit.

* * *

After graduating from college, I asked very little from my parents financially. I can still remember walking up the steps of the stage to get my diploma and feeling delighted to be an educated, free woman with opportunities to seek. My parents tended to be controlling, and graduation was a big step to becoming my own person. The days of being indebted to them or feeling dependent on their generosity were over at last.

You can call it pride, but I wanted to make my mark and do it on my own, whatever "it" was going to be. I've always been an independent person. And now the tools were there for success: education, brains, motivation, a good family upbringing, and the desire to leave the world a better place. I wasn't sure what I wanted to do, yet I knew marriage, having children, and finding my passion were on the list. There would be a journey to find that passion, I realized, but I would keep trying. In the meantime biology and chemistry were my majors at school, so a job as a chemist or biochemist was the first step. Somehow I felt that my career would eventually segue from there.

* * *

I was offered a job in chemistry at Kodak in Rochester, New York. The pay was less than what my sister was making as a secretary without a bachelor's degree. Jobs were difficult to find in 1974, so I postponed my career and made the decision to attend graduate school. It was the easiest thing to do until I could decide what career path to follow. Many young people don't know what they want to do when they graduate from college.

At the last minute, I applied to a few schools and was offered a teaching scholarship at Georgetown University in its biochemistry PhD program. It was an honor to be accepted at such a school.

However, the last thing I wanted to do was go to school for another four years. Instead, I accepted an offer at the state university in Albany to pursue my master's degree, which would take only two years. I liked chemistry but was not married to it. It was easy for me, and so I took the path of least resistance. Thus far there was no passion in any career choice for me. Time still had to unfold.

# ALL GROWN UP

*Your future depends on*
*what you do today.*

−MAHATMA GANDHI

I
n 1977 after obtaining my master's degree, I worked at Bell Labs in Murray Hill, New Jersey, as a chemist. I was fortunate to meet many people who became my friends as I learned about various equipment and was assigned research projects. Working in a lab environment taught me discipline and strategy. I worked independently, orchestrating my experiments under Dr. Schernhorn. After we did a research project, a summary was written of our research; and if good enough, it was published in journals. I believe I have two or three published articles in scientific journals relating to polymer chemistry.

About seven years before I came to Bell Labs, the big bang theory was developed at Holmdel, another Bell Labs location. Engineers working on sounds in space originally thought the static sound they heard was from faulty equipment. Later they realized it was coming from space and growing fainter as the stars moved farther apart. This was at a time when all sorts of discoveries were being made, many of them at Bell Labs.

While at Murray Hill, I was one of the early people working on coatings for optical fibers and learning that glass is one of the strongest materials. Its only flaw is its vulnerability to oxidizing, which allows the glass to develop fine cracks and shatter. If, however, a glass fiber is covered with an airtight coating immediately after being pulled from the heat, it can bend and is extremely strong.

One of the forerunners of computers was developed at Bell Labs. It was called UNIX and was a multiuser, multitasking system. Initially it was used with sixteen-bit minicomputers and took up a large, air-conditioned room with insulated floors. I remember receiving a tour of the vast air-conditioned room and being in awe of the new technology. This system managed the whole building and was spectacular. Nowadays a phone has more power. Amazing.

> **Learn as much knowledge as you can and develop a special niche. It makes you more valuable, and people will come to you for help.**

At Bell Labs I formed bonds with three friends—two men and one woman, Irene, all of whom were over sixty and close to retirement. They would go out to lunch every other Tuesday and sometimes take me with them to offer advice and friendship. It was like having three mentors.

One lesson I'll never forget and have continued to pass on to my mentees is this one from Irene: "Learn as much knowledge as you can and develop a special niche. It makes you more valuable, and people will come to you for help. Knowledge gives you control and opens up opportunities you may have missed. Yet it is empowering only when shared and when accompanied by enthusiasm."

Realizing that the position at Bell Labs was a dead end without a PhD, I started thinking about other opportunities. Bell Labs was great for a family man or woman who liked to work from nine to five and get a raise every year. Granted, many of the employees were brilliant scientists since Bell Labs attracted only the most educated and talented scientists and engineers from the best universities around the world. Yet it was too dull for me. I wanted more excitement and independence than just working in a laboratory. My brain was a perfect fit for the work, yet my heart belonged in another field.

I knew nothing about the business world or being an entrepreneur but wanted to learn as much as possible. The thrill of doing something different each day and working in a job that offered independence and leadership was enticing. Therefore, I chose to transition within the company umbrella to Bell's sister company, AT&T Long Lines.

Forty-five years ago Bell Labs, AT&T, Long Lines, Western Electric, and several smaller Bell operating companies were under one umbrella. Soon after I left Long Lines, the companies split up due to being ruled a monopoly. Working at Long Lines was my introduction to this new environment.

* * *

In 1978 I took the plunge and left chemistry and Bell Labs behind. I moved from Murray Hill, New Jersey, to White Plains, New York. My new job at AT&T Long Lines was in a sales support position. I wanted to eventually become a sales account representative responsible for working directly with the customer. My first job, as part of the support team, was more technical and involved writing up routing guides for phone systems. I was a quick study and needed no additional training, typically offered to employees entering this job. The work had little to do with business decisions or direct sales, but at least I was working in an office environment. To become an actual sales representative, you needed to take a specially designed sales test offered to people who showed ambition and promise.

My boss, George, arranged for me to take the sales test, which was not written but rather a verbal role-playing exercise. He brought me into a room and left me with three men dressed in suits and ties. To me they all looked pudgy and complacent, but memory can play games with your mind after forty years. They handed me a brochure about XYZ company, which sold tires, and gave me half an hour to read it. I knew nothing about tires, cars, or anything in between. All I knew was that you stick a key in the ignition and the car goes. If you need a new tire, you bring your vehicle to a tire repair shop, and they fix it. That was the sum of my expertise. Plus, I could not care less about tires, treads, grades, specs, or warranties.

So when the three intimidating men came into the office after precisely thirty minutes, I had gotten through only about 40 percent of the book and was confused. I knew I could have read more, but the material was so dull to me, and all I kept doing was looking at my watch and worrying. I kept wishing the topic was something I found more interesting.

The three men played the role of a distribution team looking for a tire supplier. They asked me all sorts of technical questions. All I could do was nervously reply, "I don't know the answer to that, but I can get back to you tomorrow after I research it."

In between bouts of role-playing, I would ask them how they picked the subject matter and how a half hour could be enough to study an unfamiliar subject. They shrugged with indifference. I don't think I answered one question correctly, and they stared at me disappointedly. Afterward I found out I failed the test miserably. On a scale of one to ten, I got a zero. I knew I hadn't done well, but a zero? Maybe I'm exaggerating, but the score was indeed embarrassingly low. I wasn't used to failing tests.

Thinking back now, I see it was their loss. It turns out I am a great salesperson. Yet I can only sell things that I understand. Testing me about a product that is foreign to my mind is akin to my testing them on selling electron microscopy equipment to the scientists at Bell Labs—with only thirty minutes to read up on it.

Feeling disheartened at not being promoted, I came to see the unfairness of the testing process. It was completely skewed toward a man or at least somebody who knew about tires. I was disappointed that a company the size of AT&T Long Lines was not savvy enough to offer a fair testing process for qualified salespeople.

# INTRODUCTION TO
# THE BUSINESS WORLD

*The only impossible journey*
*is the one you never begin.*

–TONY ROBBINS

Over the past twenty-plus years, many people have asked me when I realized I was an entrepreneur and how and when I eventually decided to start my present company, Aurora Products. I didn't realize I was an entrepreneur until several years after working at AT&T Long Lines and Bell Labs. My adolescent and college years were influential in helping me understand what I liked and did not like doing, yet I had a long way to go before I found my dream or even the path to my dream.

The following pages delve into adventures I have experienced in my unique journey to becoming an entrepreneur and starting my successful business. After getting married, I went into so many failed ventures, both with and without my husband. The lessons learned were fun yet exhausting. Add to that the stress of raising four children, and I often found myself reflecting on what would make me happy. But answers were not easy to find. In the bottom of my heart, however, I believed there was something out there for me.

I knew I had one primary trait—determination. Once I recognized that I had the entrepreneurial bug, the only thing standing between me and my goal was *me*. The most challenging aspect of starting Aurora Products was finding an opportunity to develop the excitement I craved in a fun and profitable business. As I stated above, many ventures that started in my early business years did not make it. Why? I believe that most, if not all, of the time and the passion and commitment for the business just weren't strong enough for success. But you only need *one* victory.

## You only need one victory.

# DETERMINATION AND HARD WORK

*Every day is a new beginning—take a deep
breath, smile, and start again.*

— WINSTON PORTER

In June 1979 while working at Long Lines, I met Richard Blackwell (Dick), who would become my first husband. He was tall, wore glasses, and had an appealing Southern accent from his childhood upbringing in Alabama. When we first met, he owned a relocation company, Key Personnel, that helped me relocate from New Jersey to New York State. Claire, one of his agents, met with me to review all the towns around White Plains and discuss demographics, finances, and school systems for each city. She then referred me to a real estate agency in Montrose, New York, the town I chose. Key Personnel made a commission on the purchase of my condo.

After the closing Dick gave me a call for a "follow-up" interview on dealing with Key Personnel. He hadn't personally met me, but he knew I was single and available. A few years after we were married, he confided to me that he had a plan for our first encounter: If I was attractive, he'd ask me out for lunch. If I had three eyes, halitosis, and black teeth, he would sit with me for the interview in one of the conference rooms and then make a hasty exit. I guess I passed the test—he asked me out to lunch. It lasted for over two hours, and a romance was started.

Key Personnel's competition was fierce, with many real estate agencies setting up relocation divisions within their companies. Dick was not enthusiastic about this business but instead looked at it as something he'd started on his own that provided him a good income. Once the company was set up, he spent little time nurturing its growth or networking but rather delegated the work to his employees.

Dick and I got married in December of the same year after a quick courtship. He was just what I was looking for at the time and the first man I ever wanted to marry. Let's just say I'd kissed a lot of frogs, and Dick was my Prince Charming—or so I thought at the time. He was smart, witty, affectionate, business oriented, and a Harvard graduate. Who could ask for a better prospect? Within a year of our marriage, I got pregnant and left Long Lines.

Unfortunately Key Personnel folded, and Dick had to accept a job in New York City. When Key Personnel went under, Dick was disappointed but not devastated since he didn't seem to have a lot of interest in working with clients and networking. He was always very open about owning his own business, but Key Personnel didn't keep his attention. Over the years Dick kept trying different avenues. In retrospect he should have been pursuing something he was enthusiastic about instead of looking at businesses purely for the sake of independence and money.

\* \* \*

Dick and I had two children within two years. The first one, Matthew, was an active little boy who just could not sit still. Laura, the second, was a very feminine baby. She had the longest fingers and toes and fulfilled my dream of having a boy and girl. Today they are both my little babies, even though they are thirty-nine and forty years old.

Dick and I pursued another avenue to start a business. We purchased thirty-three acres of land in Monroe, Connecticut, obtaining the money by leveraging our home and by taking out a business loan. The land project was called Nelson Brook Estates. Pursuing this development was Dick's idea—he needed to get out of the city. Maybe this development would segue him into a new career as a land developer? No such luck.

We started with two different opinions. I wanted to split the thirty-three-acre parcel of land into two large sections. The first section, parcel A, was on Barn Hill Road, a back road in Monroe. It was big enough for eight separate lots. Parcel B was a section of land that extended deep into the woods and required a road to be built, which would allow the subdivision to provide ground for eight additional lots. It would have been much easier to split the parcels, selling off the eight building lots we could subdivide from parcel A immediately and selling parcel B to a land developer who knew the pitfalls and procedures of building a road.

Dick insisted we do it all his way. "No, Steph, I don't want to sell off parcel B. I know I can subdivide it myself. Why share the profit with a middleman if I can do it on my own?" Dick was like the monkey with its hand stuck in the cookie jar. All he had to do was let go of the cookie, but he just couldn't do it. It was a challenging time.

Unforeseen issues arose, such as shale in the soil requiring dyna-miting the land, lack of water access to the end of the property, and a bismuth mine that the town declared a historical landmark. Of all the unlucky surprises that can occur with a piece of land, who would have thought of a bismuth mine? Bismuth is a chemical element used in various applications from cosmetics to ammunition. The mine consisted of a small hole in the ground that had been used years ago. I never got the whole story of why it was there. By the time we laid eyes on it, it had filled in over the years and become the size of a groundhog hole.

We were forced to donate the parcel to the town and construct an access path for all the tourists who would visit the mine. I don't think anybody's ever visited the site, not one single time, as a tourist destination. To this day it is overgrown with vines and thorns. Some groundhog probably found the hole and thought it would be an excellent place for him to raise his family. The only good that came from these unforeseen obstacles was the realization that you can never tell what hurdles lie ahead in pursuing a business or enterprise. "Things" come up.

Nelson Brook Road was a dead-end street constructed through parcel B. We needed to take down all the trees and dynamite an unforeseen ledge. Then we built the road, asphalted it, and thought we were finished. At the last minute, the town told us we had to put up trees along the road. Trees? We'd spent thousands of dollars cutting them all down. We were willing to plant some trees in a couple of the spartan lots, but most of the lots still had plenty of trees. The town was unwilling to bend, stating, "It's in the rules." So we planted trees with money we barely had. It was frustrating working with town rules and regulations that were just black and white without any shades of gray.

After we purchased the land, property values dipped, and we had to sell the lots at a lower price than anticipated. The only profit we made was from the tax write-off, plus maybe a few thousand extra dollars. In retrospect we would have been better off if we had split up the two parcels originally, as I had suggested.

* * *

From 1983 to 1989, to do something without Dick or the children, I began teaching chemistry and biology at local colleges, including Fairfield University, University of New Haven, Housatonic College, and the nursing program at Greenwich Hospital. Teaching allowed me to get out of the house and practice speaking English without baby talk. I loved my children dearly but always wanted a life other than simply raising kids. Working at the universities also helped keep my résumé up to speed should I choose to go back to work when the children were older. The most important reason for working was to build up some savings or pin money that I could spend any way I chose. Although the pay was poor and it was not enjoyable teaching students who typically did not like science labs, I saved every penny I earned, which eventually allowed me to purchase some small properties independently.

Our third child, Lindsay, was born in 1983. She was a surprise baby but very much wanted. Having three children was a daunting challenge and probably the most draining job I've ever had. Dick was not a hands-on father who could anticipate the needs of a child. He would do what I asked but would get frustrated and sometimes angry at the children with their demands and periodic whining. I was exhausted taking care of three babies, doing much of the legwork for the land development, and teaching part time. Dick was in New York City, working for Time-Life Video to support the family. Later in the year, he changed jobs to vice president of marketing for National Education Corp. Over the next ten years, he worked at more than seven different companies, usually as vice president or director of marketing.

In the early 1980s, real estate prices rose quickly, and I wanted to be a part of the rising wave. I bought two condos and one starter home in six years and rented them out. Owning something of my own was important to me, as I was tired of being referred to only as the wife of the household. Ever since childhood I had yearned to be recognized and respected as my own person. I'd always wanted to be independent. The real estate venture was my own business, and I alone was responsible for it.

One time after finishing up the final draft of a binder for a property I bought from the pin money I earned from teaching, the agent put Dick's name down first since he had come along with me. I said, "No. The offer is in my name only."

She looked at Dick and apologized, asking him if it was okay. "I don't want to insult you, Mr. Blackwell, so I assume this is all right with you also?" This remark further encouraged me to think about doing something on my own in the future.

\* \* \*

Sometime between building Nelson Brook Road and 1986, Dick decided to start another venture and form a company called Real-List, which would leverage the still new internet to help prospective buyers find homes. We used the money saved from his New York salaries. The concept was a great idea and a forerunner of real estate search engines like Zillow, Trulia, Redfin, and Realtor.com. Today a prospective homeowner can research homes over the internet instead of going through a real estate broker and browsing through a multiple listing book. In the 1980s, though, it was difficult to know what homes were available in a new area without contacting a broker in that area and having them send you information through the mail or discussing it with them on the phone. We have come a long way in the past thirty-five years in helping people hunt for their perfect home.

Dick's strength was never networking, nor did he understand the computer. Therefore, setting up a company as a real estate search engine was not realistic. The company never got off to a complete start due to competition and the vast undertaking required to bring the business to fruition. Real-List declared bankruptcy the first year.

\* \* \*

While I was in the thick of nesting with my three older children, my sister Valerie was also having her children. She had two boys and considered having a third and trying for a girl. She desperately wanted a daughter. I was interested in seeing if you could do anything to increase your odds of having a girl or boy and found some research performed by Dr. Ericsson. He developed a system of separating a man's sperm for the X and Y chromosomes, which determine the sex of the child. Using Dr. Ericsson's procedure, a woman's chance of having a baby of her chosen gender increased from 50 percent to a bit over 70 percent. Dr. Ericsson was offering clinics for gender selection using his technique. This piqued my interest, although it could be controversial to many people. (It is still controversial, though new techniques, performed in conjunction with IVF, have nearly perfected the process.)

Dick and I went to the OB-GYN firm that had delivered our babies to discuss the concept and see if we could create a clinic using this technique. They were excited at the prospect and met with us to move forward. Unfortunately, although Dick and I did a lot of legwork, we were informed eventually that Dr. Ericsson would release his rights only to doctors who met his criteria. Neither of us was a doctor, much less an obstetrician. However, the doctors firm we were talking with did gain the rights to Dr. Ericsson's techniques, which they added as a service for their practice.

At the time, we were disappointed. Today I understand why Dr. Ericsson's organization made the decision it did. Dr. Ericsson had spent years developing his procedures and wanted to set up his clinics with the best possible chances of success. He did not want to work with investors and nonprofessionals who were solely out to make money on their research but rather with hands-on doctors who would implement the techniques they had developed. Ericsson's people were passionate about what they had to offer, and Dick and I knew very little about OB-GYN except giving birth to babies. But we sure learned a lot in researching the prospect. I learned about not only the technical aspects of separating sex chromosomes but also the humanistic quality of those who love what they do and are committed to following their mission.

\* \* \*

In the summer of 1986, Dick and I took another stab at setting up a new company. CRE Designs was a glass etching company that would etch logos or names on glassware for promotional purposes. Money for this company once again came from savings earned by Dick. We were fortunate he had high earning power and we could save money for entrepreneurial ventures.

We obtained a small space in a large warehouse that rented out units. Luckily we could arrange an annually renewed lease. We purchased two kilns, some pallets of glasses, and the equipment for staining and etching glassware. All this equipment and inventory was taken upstairs to our unit through an old freight elevator with a scissor door. We thought we were on our way to a lucrative business.

On January 9, 1987, Gregory—our last child—was born. Another surprise. Yet he was truly a gift from God. My family was now complete—two boys and two girls. Part of me was thrilled with this little surprise—he was such a sweet little baby. Another part was impatient that his birth would postpone my plans of going out into the business world full time. It would be another five years until he started school. I remember bringing him as an infant to the glass etching company and laying him on the floor to sleep in the small office while I worked. He was only three weeks old.

Our motivation for starting CRE Designs stemmed from a meeting Dick had with a broker who assured us there was a wealth of business out there for CRE Designs and promised us the world. We were so excited at the prospect of finally owning a successful business. Unfortunately we had only one customer, the Hibernian Society. They ordered clear mugs with their logo stained on them. They were our first and last customer. CRE Designs lasted less than a year from start to finish. We liquidated the inventory and got out of our lease in 1987. Both Dick and I were disappointed and discouraged in our efforts to find a company of our own that would succeed. Everything we worked hard at setting up seemed to fail.

I learned a few important lessons though. First, always question the enthusiasm of a business broker if they have nothing to lose. They can promise you anything, but you're the one taking the risk.

The second lesson was understanding why the business folded so quickly. We had blindly started a business, knowing nothing about promotional gifts or glass etching. Most significantly we had done it without customers or prospects. We just went out and invested in equipment, inventory, and a lease, not knowing who was going to buy our service down the line.

The last lesson was that I did not like the business of etching glass and had no talent or interest in the process. It required an artistic eye and patience, which were not my strong points. I always got Cs in art class. Starting a business that does not hold your interest is a poor idea indeed.

* * *

In 1988 Dick was working for Prodigy. I was exhausted by his unhappiness at all our failures to start a successful new business. I had a yearning to do my own thing by which I could be recognized for being something more than solely a mother and wife.

Dick had always been the driving force in starting our own business and referred to himself as an entrepreneur. I never thought of myself that way, but in retrospect I realize entrepreneurship was a trait we both shared. I was not as verbal as Dick in expressing my desire for my own business yet wrote in my diary quite often about my frustrations at being stuck in a holding pattern as a stay-at-home mom. I recognized the importance of providing children with a stay-at-home parent, if possible, yet looked forward to my children being more independent, which would enable me to pursue a business or career. Our marriage was becoming more and more of a strain, as Dick continued to focus on his lack of success as an entrepreneur and I looked forward to doing something on my own.

* * *

Dick and I started several businesses and adventures together over the years. All of them eventually failed, although we did make some money in real estate. In between the endeavors listed above, we would often purchase homes, renovate them, and flip them. For example, there were two houses in Monroe on the same lot of land. We went to the town hall to split the property into two lots and then sold each house. Dealing with town hall and renovating the houses was a lot of work. In the end we lost money because the mortgage was too high to carry during the time it took us to renovate and sell. Also, the real estate market plummeted in the late 1980s, and the houses were worth less than what we paid for them.

We also purchased a few small apartment buildings, the largest having six apartments. Although we made some money from these, most of them entailed a lot of work. I recall spending many Saturdays cutting hedges, painting walls, and hauling away junk with the children in tow.

Since Dick was working in New York, I spent a lot of time collecting rent and arranging for work to be done to the apartments by contractors or ourselves and our brood of kids. I remember Dick and I taking our kids to a three-apartment home in Larchmont that we owned to cut the hedges. The kids just kept picking up thorny branches, whining, and asking when we could go home. Taking care of landholdings is not easy unless you have someone to do it for you. Yet we counted on the apartment houses' real estate values to increase so we could eventually sell them at a profit. Plus, we generated some rental income during the time we owned them.

One of the buildings Dick and I purchased was in Cheshire, Connecticut. We partnered with George and Ginny Bailey, friends of ours who were also interested in real estate. This building was old and worn down. It contained six residential apartments and two commercial units in the main building. There was another small building in the parking lot, about two hundred square feet, for the puppy spa that comprised the third commercial unit. The floors in the main building sagged from gravity taking its toll for many years. When walking from the living room to the kitchen, you felt like a drunken sailor walking on a slanted ship.

The paint was thick on the walls from all the coats applied over the years after a tenant would leave. Ginny and I would go there during weekdays when the kids were in school to change ceiling tiles or paint over dirty walls. The four of us worked every weekend fixing the building up and eventually got all the vacant units rented. The building brought in enough rent to allow both couples to take a draw each month. The apartment house in Cheshire is the only building still owned by any of us.

I took care of the Cheshire property during Ginny's battle with cancer and eventual passing. During her sickness I helped her in whatever way I could, but the end result did not change. I recall feeling remorse that she would not have the time to enjoy her independence after her kids got older—she'd had the entrepreneurial bug just as I did. I also realized that you can postpone your dreams till tomorrow, but tomorrow may never come.

After a while I had the idea that I could set up a full-service rental management company since I had gained so much knowledge and experience from Cheshire and our other rental buildings and condos. There were a lot of landlords and long-distance owners who didn't want to be bothered with building maintenance, so I thought offering such a service at affordable prices would be appreciated.

> **You must be all-in with a business, or it's not going to make it.**

This would be my own business, and I would have control of it.

I contacted as many apartment buildings and rental homes as possible without the aid of Google (which had yet to be invented), asking if they needed help managing their real estate. I got no interest. In retrospect I wasn't aggressive enough, having so much on my plate with children and other endeavors.

The lesson learned? You must be all-in with a business, or it's not going to make it.

\* \* \*

Another tactic we tried was to see if we could find a franchise to operate instead of starting a new business. Creating new companies had proved to be a challenge for us. Maybe a franchise would be the way to establish our own business? We investigated obtaining a McDonald's franchise but were shocked at the costs. You could not purchase just one store at that time but needed to buy a minimum of three. That was impossible with our cash flow. We would need to finance most of it, and I was not comfortable with such a large debt.

Next, Dick investigated getting a franchise selling blueprints for Schult homes. These prefabricated houses were expensive and made from quality materials. My parents built a Schult home on their estate, and it was beautiful. I am not sure exactly what happened with that idea, but somehow the opportunity never came to fruition. It's probably good that it didn't since we knew nothing about building homes or blueprints. Dick barely knew which direction to screw in a light bulb. I couldn't imagine him working on prefabricated homes.

The last franchise we investigated was a Little Caesars pizza franchise. Rather than establish a new location, we found an existing franchise in Orange, Connecticut, that was willing to sell. We needed the funds to purchase it and the willingness to work. Last but not least, we needed to know how to make pizza. I am not a big pizza lover, but I was willing to learn how to make it for others. The first day I went into the facility, the owner showed me the art of making a good pizza, heating the oven, and managing the store if an employee did not show up, which was often.

Bottom line, the owner needed to be prepared to jump in and run the place, no matter what time of the day or evening. I had no interest in being called to go make pizza at 7:00 p.m. on a Sunday while sitting by the fireplace with my four children. Dick had little interest in making pizza either yet was attracted by the business aspects. He envisioned owning three or four branches. This was not going to work, though, and I drew the line. I could not see myself with a chef's hat on my head and flour on my apron. I was not Mama Pizza, nor did I want to smell like garlic. Chanel No. 5 was my choice of body scent. We decided not to pursue this business.

* * *

Upon reflection Dick and I were very busy after getting married in 1979. We had four children, moved homes three times, worked at several jobs, and encountered numerous hurdles in finding a business that would offer him success and me a sense of passion and fulfillment. We started Key Personnel Inc., Nelson Brook Road Development, Real-List, and CRE Designs and purchased several houses, condos, and apartments for renovation or investment. We also investigated starting up a gender selection clinic, a prefab house business, and a pizza franchise. I was getting tired of all the challenges and didn't want the family to suffer. It takes its toll on marriages. We had the energy and drive; we just needed that one success.

I've heard that perseverance means enduring not one long struggle but rather a string of battles. If you fall, get up. Lord knows we did a lot of falling in those ten years. As Marie Curie put it, "Life is not easy for any of us. But what of that? We must have perseverance and, above all, confidence in ourselves. We must believe that we are gifted for something and that this thing must be attained."

# AMALGAMATED PRODUCE INC.

## *Our First Success*

*Don't worry about failure;
you only have to be right once.*

—DREW HOUSTON

**D**ick looked through the papers and talked to business brokers every day, looking for opportunities. Social media and online search engines were not readily available in the eighties, so hunting was not easy. In March of 1989, Dick came to tell me he had found a great opportunity—a business for sale—advertised in the *Wall Street Journal*. It was located close to our hometown of Fairfield, Connecticut. At that time, he was well into his forties and anxious to have his own business. Finding one had turned out to be a greater struggle than he'd anticipated, and he saw the years flying by without fulfilling his dream. For me I thought, *Here we go again, a lot of work and anxiety in buying a company and hoping it succeeds.*

My husband was a true entrepreneur and did not want to work for anybody else. But I told him I did not want to go this route again. Still after much persuasion, I agreed, with the provision that if this company did not work out, he would stop trying to purchase or start any new companies at the family's expense and find happiness somewhere else. I felt our life together was like sitting on a seesaw. And with four young children, we couldn't keep losing money on new endeavors.

I was tired and had my own career to consider. The kids were getting older, and I hoped to find something I was passionate about. I was unsure if I wanted to start a business of my own or take on a job that allowed independence. What I did know was that I did not want to do it with Dick. We had done too many things together, and I was tired. My reservoir of patience was running low, and our marriage was shaky. This would be the last hurrah.

The company's name was Amalgamated Produce Inc. (sometimes referred to as API or Amalgamated). It sold alfalfa sprouts under the brand Specialty Farms. An important stipulation in purchasing Amalgamated Produce was that Dick had to agree that we would go into this venture with another couple looking to sell their small sprout business called Lively Bites. We were introduced to them by our broker. Jim and his wife, the owners of Lively Bites, were anxious to get out of their flailing business. If we merged, they would own about 11 percent of the new company. From my perspective, this was a great opportunity because we wouldn't be going into a business blindsighted but instead with someone who had experience and knew the ropes. Jim would assume the role of production manager, and his wife would remain a silent partner.

The business broker was a difficult person for me to deal with because he assumed Dick and Jim would be running the business solo, regardless of what he was told. I informed him of both Dick's and my involvement in purchasing the business from the very beginning. Yet the broker continued to leave both wives out of all conversations and negotiations.

After a few meetings in which the broker failed to address me, I lost my patience and blurted out, "Unless you give me respect and eye contact in these negotiations, you will not be allowed in my home. I am tempted to pull out of the whole deal."

His answer? "I'm sorry for insulting you, but from my experience, women don't usually run businesses. However, they are indeed important because they can ruin the negotiations if they don't want their husbands purchasing a business." I refused to have him back in the house, and he met Dick at the Hi-Ho Motel in town to finalize the contracts.

We purchased the company for about $430,000. Since we had very little money in the bank, we leveraged our home and other assets to purchase the business "via paper," with the sellers acting as the bank. Dick had the old-school training at Harvard, where they taught students to leverage other people's money. In purchasing past businesses, his first thought for obtaining funds was to borrow. If we borrowed a hundred thousand dollars, Dick would regard it as newfound money at our disposal. I would think, *Oh dear, another loan to repay.* I've always felt uncomfortable borrowing money and will always avoid loans as much as possible.

> **I've always felt uncomfortable borrowing money and will always avoid loans as much as possible.**

The company was a hydroponic farm that grew alfalfa sprouts in large, rotating drums sprinkled with water every sixty seconds. Thirty-two pounds of seed were put into each drum, and four days later, after being rotated, watered, and exposed to UV light, three hundred pounds of sprouts were harvested. They were then plunged into a large tank filled with cold water, washed, spun dry, and then hand-packed in plastic containers by a line of employees. After the sprouts sat in the refrigerator for twenty-four hours, we loaded them onto pallets and delivered the pallets to the customer's warehouse to be distributed to each store.

\* \* \*

Before purchasing the business, Dick worked with the numbers and came up with some projections based on raising our prices and offering different types of sprouts. In those days there was no such thing as Excel or even Lotus 123. Projections and spreadsheets were all done by hand.

According to Dick and our accountant, our sales were projected to increase by 10 percent. I thought skeptically, *Yeah, right.* I did not believe it and have always hated projections. Numbers on a page cannot foretell the future or predict problems you might encounter in a new arena. Who could have foreseen the bismuth mine on the property we developed in Monroe? Things happen that you don't expect. I was concerned about the company's survival because we were leveraged to the gills and had experienced so many failures in the past. However, Dick was determined that his dream of owning a business would come true, and he was an optimist.

\* \* \*

From the very beginning, Amalgamated could not support us. Our projections were off, and sales did not increase by 10 percent. In fact, they initially fell by about 20 percent due to competition and the loss of a major customer. Also, when sprouts had first come out ten years earlier, they were something new and generated enthusiasm as a nice topping on a salad or sandwich. After a while consumers no longer considered them unique but rather just another item on the shelf.

From the very beginning, it was difficult for us to pay employees and purchase inventory. Consequently Dick continued working for Prodigy, his latest employer in New York City, and was one of the many people who stood by the train tracks every morning. I, in turn, ran the business. I understood his disappointment and was sympathetic when he complained. We both had a lot of stress from running the business and supporting a family of six. Also, the children were still very young. I respected him for his commitment to taking care of our family financially. Any profit we made from Amalgamated was poured into paying off the immense debt we'd incurred in purchasing the business.

* * *

Amalgamated Produce was located in Norwalk, and it had three years remaining on its lease. The building was in a safe area and offered easy access to the highway, which took me home in twenty-five minutes. It was the first business on the right as you entered the industrial park, and we leased around nine thousand square feet. The park owner didn't particularly like us as tenants because our dumpster, which stood at the entrance to the industrial park, stunk from rotting sprout waste. In addition, the water and humidity from our production process was rusting the ceiling of her building, and she was concerned about the accelerated wear and tear.

The children's ages ranged from three to nine when we first moved in, so they spent a lot of time at the company with us on weekends while we worked inside. They would jump on pallets, play in the lofts, take out the garbage, and walk across the nearby railroad tracks to a small candy store as a treat. Sometimes they would put coins on the tracks to see them flattened like pancakes. Occasionally we may have gotten the three eldest children to do a little bit of work. But after fifteen minutes, they would somehow disappear, only to be found in the office putting their faces on the copy machine glass and taking pictures of funny expressions.

I enjoyed working in a business that I could manage, yet I did not feel any enthusiasm for the product we grew. The growing room smelled of humidity, sprouts, and chlorine from sterilizing the drums between cycles. Most of my clothes had bleach spots from rubbing against surfaces that had just been cleaned or grease spots from the lubrication used in the gears for the drums. I recall my mother saying, "Stephanie, you're a thirty-eight-year-old woman. You're old enough to dress well. You need more clothes instead of the same khaki pants and shirt."

I would impatiently answer, "Mom, half the time I'm at the company dealing with sprouts, water, grease, and chlorine. The other half I spend with children who constantly wipe their dirty hands on my pants or with a baby who regurgitates milk on my shoulder."

I didn't have much time to attend Junior League meetings, PTA functions, or Garden Club luncheons. Most of my time was spent working at Amalgamated Produce or with the kids. Overall I enjoyed staying busy and preferred this lifestyle to belonging to clubs or volunteer organizations. Yet it was stressful at times.

* * *

Dick and I owned 89 percent of the controlling shares of Amalgamated Produce. I worked about thirty hours a week, and Jim worked forty hours as production manager. Despite the hard work and challenging environment, I liked the people, the mental stimulation, and the learning curve. I understood Dick's frustration at watching me run our company and live his dream, but his earning power was so much greater than mine at the time, and we had a family to support.

At the end of the year, our tax accountant told us Amalgamated Produce had made a small profit. I could not understand it since we could barely pay our bills. Dick did not collect a salary at API, and my compensation was minimal, yet we made a profit? That was when the accountant explained that much of our gain was going toward the hefty six-figure loans we'd incurred in purchasing the business. Interest rates in 1989 were around 10 percent, which in today's world is almost inconceivable. If we made $300,000 profit, $160,000 went toward principal and interest, resulting in a cash flow of $140,000. Some of this money was tied up in inventory and receivables, thereby leaving us the remaining amount. It was tough supporting a family on our income. I was determined never to be so leveraged again.

The 1990 oil price shock did not help matters. Diesel fuel for our trucks was never costlier. Yet we technically made a profit and had to pay taxes on money we never got to put into our pockets. It seemed to me that, year after year, we were constantly robbing Peter to pay Paul. Our finances at home were extremely tight. That burdensome loan with such a staggering interest rate made life difficult.

Eventually after about two years, Dick got laid off from Prodigy and never looked back to working for someone else again. He joined me at API, and we made a meager living after cutting expenses and letting go of some people, including our production manager. It was not easy terminating Jim's employment since he owned 11 percent of the company, yet we had no choice if we were to survive. We needed his salary to pay Dick and me. Eventually we bought Jim out. Dick handled general business affairs and worked on getting up to speed on production. It was a lean time for us and very stressful.

# TRIALS AND TRIBULATIONS

*To be successful, you have to have your heart in
your business and your business in your heart.*

—THOMAS WATSON SR.

After three years when Amalgamated's lease ran out, we decided to move our plant to Bridgeport, Connecticut, allowing us easy access to unskilled labor. We found an old building on Kossuth Street that needed to be retrofitted for growing sprouts. Previously the building had been used as an auto warehouse. Through Dick's perseverance we were able to get a Connecticut gift grant for over a hundred thousand dollars, enabling us to move and prepare the building. He excelled at knowing where funds were available and pursuing them. Without these funds I don't see how we possibly could have moved. Lowell Weicker was governor and did not require us to pay back the grant money.

In the summer of 1992, Dick spent most of his time at the new building sawing through concrete to make drainage ditches for the runoff water from growing the sprouts. I also worked on getting the new building in shape by painting and cleaning. We both worked hard at continuing the business in Norwalk while preparing the building in Bridgeport, about thirty miles east. Moving all the growing drums and other equipment was quite an ordeal, but by September 1992, we started operations in our new home. A loading dock was installed so our trucks could back in, which permitted pallet loading at floor level. We also gained three thousand square feet of space versus Norwalk.

Amalgamated Produce was in an economically run-down area. The company was small, with only twenty-five employees, and its dirty twelve-thousand-square-foot building was surrounded by serpentine fencing with razor wire on top. We would often come to the office to find graffiti on the exterior walls or the trucks. We supplied a lot of business to the painter down the street, who would come and whitewash the walls. The road had Jersey barriers on each block to discourage crime and occasional pit bulls walking the streets.

I was amazed we did not have more problems with the gangs, but I think the fact that we employed many neighbors helped protect us. No one wanted to kill the golden goose at a time when jobs were so hard to find. We would not have gotten the grant had we not moved to the location we chose. The city of Bridgeport was anxious to bring businesses and employment to its people, and it encouraged Amalgamated Produce to stay. Many of our employees could walk to work, and we met some kind, good-hearted people as employees.

* * *

During my years at Amalgamated Produce, I continued to learn about business aspects such as slotting allowances at retail stores, trucking, personal property taxes and exemptions, profit/loss, grants, loans, payroll issues, employee issues, general ledgers, marketing tools, etc. Some of my experiences included learning the hard way.

For example, after we purchased the business, I received a personal tax bill with an exemption form to be filled out for manufacturing companies. Not realizing that taxes were paid ahead instead of afterward, I put the documents in an envelope to be given to the previous owner, believing they pertained to the business before our purchase. Unfortunately it was not until the submission date had expired that I realized the tax forms were intended for the present owners of Amalgamated Produce. Overlooking this deadline was costly.

Dick and I pleaded with the tax assessor for an extension, telling him that we just bought the company and that the oversight was not intentional. His response? "Ignorance is no excuse in the business world." He was right, and the mistake cost us thousands of dollars. It was a lesson I never forgot.

Not only did I learn a lot about business during these years, but at the age of thirty-eight, I was in the best physical condition of my life. Since money was tight, we could not afford a production manager. As a result I would double in that role and do a lot of physical work such as seeding the drums, packing the sprouts in consumer trays, and palletizing the product delivered to warehouses the following day. I wondered why I had not lost all the weight after giving birth to my last child, but as I think it over now, I realize that muscle weighs more than body fat. Growing sprouts is labor intensive.

* * *

Several memorable people from Amalgamated come to mind now, offering a glimpse of our culture. Henry, an African American man, was our vegetable "washman" who cleaned the sprouts. He was of medium height with the body of a superhero. His arms were the thickness of my thighs, and I do not have the thinnest of thighs. This man was a workhorse. He would pick up armfuls of sprouts from bins, throw them into the twelve-foot-long vegetable tub, and collect them at the other end. He would then dump them into the vegetable dryer that spun the water off. He worked so hard yet earned only a little above minimum wage, which was all we could afford.

One day he came to work with a rag tied around the top of his head, holding his jaw closed. "Henry," I said, "what happened?"

He responded that he had a toothache but could not afford to have it pulled. He did not ask me for help, but we could not watch him suffer and sent him home to a dentist. API paid the bill.

One forty-year-old man, Norman, worked at API for a few years. He was intellectually challenged, and even though it took him a while to learn something, once he understood a task, he worked hard at it. One day his supervisor was snippy and barked at him. He boldly retorted back, "I may have no money or a big job, but I am a *man* and deserve respect! Don't talk to me as if I am less than that."

Somehow that story has stuck with me through the years. After his wife passed away, he became an addict and was eventually terminated from Amalgamated. His wife had been his caretaker. She had made sure he went to work every day and had given him reason to live. He died a few years later from drugs and alcohol. His kids were put in foster care, and then who knows what happened?

I remember Norman not only because of his insistence on being regarded with respect but also because of his desire to have his kids enjoy a better life. In 1994 we had a Christmas holiday party for all twenty-five employees with their families. Santa Claus came and delivered toys for the children. Norman had a huge grin on his face when his children got a gift. Upon leaving he thanked us, stating that he had very little money to spend on presents. He remembered receiving only one toy as a child—a GI Joe doll.

Being in an impoverished section of town and having very little cash for wages did not allow us easy access to the cream of the labor crop. So when we found someone sharp and motivated, we seized the opportunity to hire them. Adrianna was one such person. She was only nineteen years old, stunning, and a spitfire. When she first came to Amalgamated Produce from Colombia, she wore tight yellow pants, a low-cut colorful top, and an abundance of makeup. Yet behind her beauty and questionable dress style at work, Adrianna was sharp. She only had to be told once to do something. Her follow-up and leadership skills were excellent, and she soon became the production boss. We depended on Adrianna immensely and owed her a lot of gratitude for making the operation run more efficiently.

Eventually she moved on to dental hygiene. It was a loss for Amalgamated Produce. For years afterward she would touch base with me. We were like a family.

Jean, our only office employee, was an African American woman from the inner city. She was about forty-five years old when she came for her interview, and I still remember what she said. "If you give me this chance, you will never be sorry, and I will give you 100 percent." We never were. Jean was as loyal to me as they come.

Years later after I left Amalgamated Produce, Jean retired. I saw her a few times after that, and she had changed. It appeared as if life had taken its toll on her, and she was tired. It was sad to see, but we had shared some good laughs and a lot of hard work in keeping Amalgamated Produce together.

\* \* \*

Being in business with Dick was difficult for both of us since we had marital strains at home that were sometimes carried into the office. Working together at Amalgamated Produce and raising four children at home accelerated the issues through the summer of 1991. Eventually the problems led to a divorce in the winter of 1993. Despite our divorce we remained friendly and continued to work together.

I learned to be involved in everything as much as possible, recognizing that knowledge helped me become less dependent on others. I knew our software and finances, sales, production, trucking routes, and vendors. Of course, the business was small, with less than one million dollars in annual sales (equivalent to about two million dollars today), and it is easier to know all facets of a small company. As a company grows, you need to depend more and more on the people who work for you. The tasks become more complex and harder to manage, and you cannot do everything.

Dick shared with me the marketing knowledge he'd gained while working at Procter and Gamble in his younger years. I had an innate feel for sales and marketing and benefited from his formal knowledge. It helped me later when I moved on to my own company. I enjoyed learning graphic design on my own as software programs were developed in the mid-nineties, and we started making our own sell sheets and promotional material. Prior to that we would pay an outside company to make prototype labels and marketing materials. Any alterations in color or font would require expensive and time-consuming overlays. Computers were becoming more and more widespread in businesses, but not everyone had one.

Amalgamated Produce had only one computer for the main office, which we used for QuickBooks accounting software and order entry. It cost over two thousand dollars, which was a lot of money for us. The internet was not widespread, so we used only prepackaged software. Scanners did not exist, or if they did, I never knew about them, and most small businesses did not have them. Faxes were the latest invention for transferring information quickly.

I remember the first time I started using a word processor instead of a typewriter. It made such a big difference. My typing was slow and error filled, so this was a godsend, allowing me to express myself much more quickly and accurately. My writing skills had never been a strong point in school since my handwriting was slow and laborious, but suddenly I could put words together much faster and became quite articulate on paper. Dick was a bit slower in acclimating to a word processor, but he picked it up after some instructions from me. One or two years later, we both got computers and continued to move forward with technology.

* * *

For deliveries we had a large, refrigerated box truck that today would require a driver with a commercial driver's license (CDL). In the 1980s and 1990s, a CDL was unnecessary for the truck we owned or leased. Deliveries *had* to be made, especially with sprouts that were highly perishable. Plus, we could not afford to lose any sales. So if a driver could not make it, Dick would often make the delivery. However, more than once the task was delegated to me. From my perch high in the truck's driver's seat, the cars below looked so small and insignificant. I often mused how easy it would be to wipe them off the road without noticing. Thankfully that never happened. At least I don't *think* it did.

Amalgamated Produce did not have a lot of money, so our trucks were always old and worn down. I never had confidence that they would complete the journey. My biggest fear was of being stranded on the side of the road in a giant vehicle with nobody to help me. At every bump and noise, I would cringe, hoping the box wouldn't fall off the truck or the engine wouldn't die. To this day I still dream of driving a big truck and the engine stalling in some isolated spot on the highway or in a dangerous neighborhood. Cell phones were not readily available during those early years. I would have had a much more relaxing ride, knowing that help was just a touch-tone away.

When I would arrive at the supermarket warehouse, I'd be shaking with nervousness as I backed into the loading dock, trying not to hit anything. When I got inside, the men in the receiving area were usually nice and helped me unload the truck. I'm not sure that would be the case today since warehouses use lumpers who are paid to unload the vehicle so as to prevent any truckers from entering the warehouse. Often lumpers and truckers belong to separate unions and are very strict about the rules of unloading.

\* \* \*

One day our driver called in the wee hours of the morning, saying he couldn't make the delivery. Dick couldn't make the run for some reason, so I hopped out of bed at three thirty, drove to Amalgamated Produce, dragged myself into the vehicle, and started on my way to make the delivery myself. It was my first time going to Hunts Point Produce Terminal, New York City's huge produce distribution hub. Big trucks and rigs were coming in to make deliveries, and smaller trucks or vans were driving out with their fresh veggies and fruits for their stores and restaurants. Outside the terminal, women of the night stood on the curbs, looking for truckers who might need a bit of "relaxation" during their early morning run.

I drove through the gate, keeping my head down as much as possible, and made my delivery in haste. Luckily all I got were stares. I felt a wave of relief as I pulled out of the terminal gate and stepped on the gas to accelerate out of the neighborhood as quickly as possible, praying the rickety truck would not break down. It's amazing to what lengths people will go to ensure the success of their business.

One of our truck drivers was robbed at gunpoint while standing at a phone booth on the corner of our street. He had left his key inside the factory and needed to call our home before sunrise so that one of us, preferably Dick, would get out of bed to let him into the factory to load his truck. One minute we heard him telling his tale of losing his key; the next minute his talk switched to "Hey, man… whoa! Yeah… yeah… here it is! Please leave me alone now." As he was standing on the corner, making his call, a man had come up behind him with a gun and demanded his wallet. That driver never lost track of his keys again, and I was careful not to enter the area in the wee hours of the morning. If I did, I always looked over my shoulder.

* * *

I was raised by a father who demanded orderliness and a proactive approach. I was much like my dad, making sure equipment was fixed before it was broken, the roof repaired before it leaked, and cleanliness constantly maintained. Dick's approach was the antithesis of mine; he felt no money should be spent unless necessary. In other words, if it's working, don't fix it. So pest control was overlooked, even though we were in the depths of the inner city.

One day while sitting in the office after the production staff left, Jean and I were chitchatting. The office door leading into the production area was open as she slowly pointed her finger at the vegetable washing machine. "Look," she said in a whisper.

Under the machine, nibbling seeds, was an animal the size of a small cat. "Eew!" I yelped and was disgusted to see that it was a rat. He was quietly enjoying his food and lapping up the water.

First thing the next day, we called Orkin, our local pest control company. Keeping up with the vermin turned out to be a daunting task since rats and mice were indigenous to the neighborhood, and roaches infested most of the buildings around us. After that first visit from the rat, we were constantly fighting battles with unwelcome pests and keeping vigil against their entry from outside.

\* \* \*

Raising children and running a business at the same time can be trying. We were very tight financially, having lost money in the housing crash of the late eighties, which affected the rental properties we owned. It was difficult to survive on the meager cash flow provided by Amalgamated. Once in a blue moon, I had no choice but to leave a sick child home for a few hours so that I could check in on everyone at work and make sure everything was running smoothly.

One day my younger daughter, Lindsay, who was about eleven years old, had a slight cold. She was recovering from a broken leg and had been wearing a cast for five weeks. Her leg was healing fine, although she needed to use crutches to help her walk.

I decided to let her stay home since I did not have a sitter. She did not seem too ill and wanted to watch TV in my bed for three hours while Mommy was away. It was a treat for her to relax in my bed, watching cartoons, and she did not seem concerned. While I was at work, I called and told her I would be coming home, asking if she wanted any burgers from Burger King.

"Oh yes, Mommy, but please come home. I miss you, and my hands are pale." Lindsay was a bit of a Sarah Bernhardt, a French actress in the late nineteenth and early twentieth centuries known for her propensity to stay in the dramatic limelight. Ever since she was a young child, Lindsay was prone to exaggerate and even expressed a strong interest in entering the theater when she got older. I told her I was leaving work right away and would be home shortly with food.

When I got home, an ambulance was parked at the front door, and Lindsay looked embarrassed and scared. Apparently during my drive home, a woman had called the house, asking for me, and Lindsay said, "She's not here. My veins are popping out of my hands, and I broke my leg." So the woman called 911.

The EMTs left as soon as I arrived but not until after I hid my head in shame for leaving my child alone for three hours. The veins on her hands were from her skin being so light and pale, and her broken leg from a skiing accident was 80 percent healed and in a cast. The paramedics recognized that and let it be. If this were to happen today, I would probably have the Connecticut Department of Children and Families (DCF) knocking on my door.

*  *  *

There are often critical control points in a food business. A critical control point is a procedure in production where preventive measures can help prevent a food safety hazard. For us refrigeration was a critical control point in maintaining the sprouts. After harvesting the fragile sprouts, we immediately packed the product and put it in our walk-in refrigerator. Boxes were separated at least an inch apart to allow air to circulate between them. In this configuration, the product in the middle of the pallet could cool down quickly. If sprouts stayed warm for too long, they would begin to deteriorate.

Our second critical control point was keeping the growing room and drums, along with all equipment used in harvesting and processing, sanitized. In growing sprouts it is imperative to maintain cleanliness to prevent product contamination. Growing produce hydroponically creates a humid environment that allows enteric bacteria to thrive. If bacteria find a home in the growing room, you are doomed for the whole crop or more. Another avenue for bacterial growth is when a drum stops rotating and the heat from the lamps enhances the production of methane gas from the sprouts. This methane, along with the humidity, creates a perfect environment for bacteria and subsequent spoilage. There is nothing more disappointing than to enter the growing room in the morning and smell the odor of manure or rotting plants.

Each drum of finished sprouts was worth quite a bit of money. At Amalgamated Produce we could ill afford the loss of revenue. If contamination occurred, not only would we lose the crop but we also would have to purchase sprouts from competitors to service our customers. After seeing the devastation in our growing room, we would throw all the product in the dumpster with a heavy lump in our throats and then chlorinate the heck out of the drums and aggressively sanitize the whole room. Sometimes the bacteria would get into the air-conditioning vents in the growing chamber, and we would have to scrub down the ducts as well.

My daughter Laura tells me she remembers when she was ten or eleven years old opening up old packages of decaying sprouts and emptying them in the dumpster. As an adult looking back on the experience, she recalls, "The smell was horrific, smelled like rotten butt."

If we were lucky after a cleaning, the next crop would be healthy. But it would often take a couple of cycles to work through it. Your heart would sink when you opened the door to the drum and were greeted by a nasty smell and brown muck. The seed was expensive, and you needed a healthy crop to sell to stores.

I know we were not alone. Periodically we would get calls from competitors asking if we had some spare product to sell. We knew what it meant without asking. Since crop loss was a common problem, sprout growers helped one another without gouging the price, with the expectation that the courtesy would be reciprocated should an issue arise on their side. Sometimes we had to go to two or three competitors to get enough sprouts to cover our orders.

* * *

When we purchased Amalgamated Produce, there were several surprises or disappointments. The first was the misunderstanding that we could add other varieties of sprouts, such as onion or garlic sprouts, to our product line. We thought this would increase our sales volume and profit. Little did we know that these two new items were slow sellers and barely affected our sales.

The second disappointment was the discovery that we could not raise our prices. When we purchased the business, the business broker and seller told us we could raise the price of our retail pack from $4.75 to $5.25. That was a significant increase, and Dick and I believed them both. So after the closing, we wrote letters to our customers informing them of price increases. Shortly after sending out these notices, orders significantly dropped, and we received calls from our customers, saying, "Thank you, but I can get sprouts from Snow Sprouts for four dollars a case."

So not only were we not able to raise pricing but we also had to lower them to compete with the new guy on the block that offered rock-bottom pricing. Snow Sprouts was owned by a Korean family that used family members to pack the product and had very little overhead. It took a couple of years to work our way back up to $4.75.

One person who helped us change our selling strategy and outlook was a competitor. We were members of the regional Sprout Association, where sprout growers got together annually to commiserate on issues as friendly competitors. We were all complaining about how difficult it was to sell our sprouts when pricing was so low. We were killing one another by lowering our prices; none of us was making money.

Barb, one of the top growers and a leader of the association, stressed that pricing is only an indicator of value. "If you feel your sprouts are of higher quality, safer, and better than someone else's, then you should expect more money. Not all apples are alike. Would you pay the same for a crab apple as you would for a juicy McIntosh? The same thing goes for sprouts." This advice was very important to me in subsequent endeavors and has stayed with me to this day. It is the value of the product consumers should look for, not only the price.

## Pricing is only an indicator of value.

The third disappointment for Amalgamated Produce was the realization that it was a regional business that was challenging, if not impossible, to grow nationally. All regions had sprout growers since it was an easy business to start up. The costs of equipment and setup were reasonably low, and therefore, competition was plentiful. Growers would sell locally and deliver product in their refrigerated trucks. It was out of the question to pursue a customer in another part of the country. Freight alone would be prohibitive, mainly because you needed refrigeration for an inexpensive, light item.

\* \* \*

Amalgamated Produce's introduction to the Occupational Safety and Health Organization (OSHA) was not a happy one. When an OSHA representative comes knocking on the door, your knees start knocking as well. Often, though not always, they come to visit based on a complaint about a violation. Usually a disgruntled employee makes a simple call to OSHA, and—voila!—they are at your facility. Rarely, if ever, has OSHA visited us without levying one or more fines. They always find something and often disagree with one another regarding violations. For example, one agent told us that we did not need an eyewash at our facility since there were hoses all over. The next agent fined us for not having the eyewash.

Our first visit was due to a complaint received by OSHA from Brian, a twenty-year-old man who worked for us for a couple of years. He was our maintenance manager and repairman. In other words, he was our only employee who was able to fix machines and lighting. Brian decided to quit and go on to greener pastures. There was some confusion about his last paycheck. After we thought we'd satisfied his questions, he walked out. Apparently he either didn't understand or didn't like what he heard. So he decided to express his dissatisfaction by calling OSHA on us.

When OSHA took a walk through our facility, they found electric tools on the floor, ceiling lighting hanging loose without covers, ungrounded plugs, and many other issues. Dick and I were appalled for two reasons. The first was a feeling of betrayal since all the problems we were being fined for were Brian's responsibilities, and he had put us in a vulnerable spot.

The other reason was that OSHA was right. We had a lot of work ahead of us to get up to speed. Ungrounded electrical cords in a wet environment growing hydroponic sprouts are hazardous—shame on us. Three lessons were learned: get a responsible maintenance person to keep your employees and facility safe, avoid OSHA violations as much as possible, and beware of disgruntled employees.

\* \* \*

One time after we had an infection of our sprouts, Dick and I were at our wits' end, trying to meet orders and make ends meet. We were struggling to get over the hump when one of our two drivers sheepishly entered the office and said, "Um… Dick… I need to tell you I had a slight accident down the road and need someone to help tow me out."

Slight? After one of his runs, he decided to go to the local pub for a beer and then took a shortcut under a low-lying railroad bridge. You can imagine what happened next. Yup, crash! The truck was too high, and the top was shaved off until it became jammed under the trestle. Luckily we had insurance.

One week later this guy came into the office looking for his paycheck—yes, after destroying his employer's truck on the heels of a beer stop. According to the state of Connecticut, though, we owed him his pay, so we gave him his paycheck and a pink termination slip to go along with it.

\* \* \*

As mentioned earlier Amalgamated Produce was a local business where you eventually run out of new customer prospects. There are only so many supermarket chains within a three-hundred-mile radius. So most, if not all, sprout growers branched out to offer other items.

One competitor started a vegetable juice company called Fresh Samantha. Eventually the juice company became far more profitable than the sprout business and was sold to Odwalla. Another sprout company offered organic vegetables in addition to their sprouts. Others added mung bean sprouts to their assortment. At Amalgamated Produce we also branched out.

Product expansion was a primary interest of mine. I loved researching new products and thinking of new ideas and options.

In the summer of 1993, we were selling a product that contained an assortment of mixed beans. We would soak the beans for twenty-four hours, strain off the water, and package them as "crunchy pea mix." By the time the customer purchased the mix at the supermarket, the beans would be slightly sprouted and could be used as a topping for salads. Since we carried these beans in-house, I thought, *Why not make a dried bean soup mix? I could hire a co-packer to make up individual spice packets, and we could insert one packet into each package of dried beans, print a recipe on the back, and sell it as Homestyle Bean Mix.* I thought it was a creative idea.

We decided to try it. We were able to get this mix into a couple of stores. Next, I thought, *Why not try Costco or BJ's Wholesale Clubs?* I was too naive to be intimidated or to understand the logistics of packaging, shipping, demo costs, or anything else for large warehouse clubs. All I knew was that they were not carrying any dried bean soup mixes at the time and that it was a good idea. So I found out who the buyer was at Costco, called him, and prepared my sample to bring with me. I figured they would be interested in a family-sized container, so I decided a sixty-four-ounce jar would look good.

When I walked into the buyer's office in my suit, looking professional, I wondered if he knew he was the first warehouse buyer I had ever met. Anyway he loved the product and was willing to work with me to develop packaging and pallet configurations. I got the product into the Northeast region, and it was a success for over two years. This success helped keep Amalgamated Produce afloat and gave me experience for future endeavors.

Dealing with a highly perishable, humid item was not fun for me, and I was determined to offer more shelf-stable items to supermarkets. I had no interest in sprouts and didn't even like eating them. I did, however, enjoy all the new things we were introducing and took delight in learning how to put together sell sheets and promotional materials for products I stood behind.

\* \* \*

After the soup medley's introduction to supermarket chains, we also added wild rice, dried cranberries, dried cherries, and dried blueberries to our line. Prior to the 1990s, dried berries were primarily limited to raisins, and people loved the introduction of blueberries, cranberries, cherries, and other berries. The difference between raisins and dried cranberries, besides the fruit, is that raisins are just harvested and dried. Cranberries are frozen, infused with sugar, and dried. Consumers loved dried cranberries, and the item continues to be popular in supermarket chains to this day. Dried blueberries and cherries, although more expensive, are also in demand.

Dried mushrooms were entering the market too, so we decided to add them to our offerings. They were an interesting item but prone to meal moths. All produce has its weakness. At least these new items did not have to be refrigerated, and all we needed to do was keep them away from flies and insects that love fruit, veggies, and mushrooms. Easier said than done.

One time when introducing our latest item to a supermarket buyer, I showed him our assortment of dried mushrooms. When I pulled out the dried porcini, he turned the clear package upside down and said, "Hello, little fella. Nice to meet you." I was aghast with embarrassment as I noticed he was talking to a meal moth climbing around inside the package.

Earlier I had grabbed a sample of mushrooms sitting in my office to give to the buyer without examining it for quality. Who knows how long it had been sitting there? He seemed amused, but I think it was half an hour before my face turned from crimson back to normal.

From then on I always made sure all samples sent to buyers were freshly made and of impeccable quality.

In addition to getting the soup mix into Costco, we also managed to get two additional items on the shelf, wild rice and cranberry stuffing and dried cranberries. The stuffing mix incorporated dried cranberries and quick-cook wild rice that we carried in-house. We purchased the seasoned stuffing wholesale from Pepperidge Farms, which was nearby.

All three projects—the soup mix, the stuffing, and the cran-berries—were developed and marketed by me since research and development, as well as sales, were my skills. I loved the part of my job that involved thinking of new products we could introduce to the market. Dick enjoyed running the finances and operations, which were his strengths.

# TRANSITIONING
# AWAY

*Any transition is easier if you
believe in yourself and your talent.*

—PRIYANKA CHOPRA

The years 1993 to 1995 were very lean for me. I lived on child support and whatever meager money Amalgamated Produce could afford to pay. After the divorce from Dick, I moved out of our beautiful colonial home in Fairfield and moved to a less expensive house in the country. I received no alimony unless you consider one dollar per year alimony. Yet I was happier on my own. As a husband Dick had alternated between Dr. Jekyll and Mr. Hyde. He was not the man I fell in love with and thought I married, and I felt free without him.

My four children refused to share bedrooms. The two girls were completely different and needed their space. The two boys were six years apart, making it difficult for them to share. Finding a home that offered five bedrooms was difficult, but after much searching, I finally did it. I bought a four-bedroom house and converted the downstairs study into a bedroom for my older son. (Little did I know the exit door within his room would provide him a means of sneaking out in the night to see his girlfriend when he got older.)

The only health insurance I could afford for the kids and myself was catastrophic coverage should something major happen. For checkups or colds, I took my children to the walk-in clinic in the middle of Bridgeport, along with other people who shared my economic status at the time. I remember my wealthy cousin Vicki coming to my house with a bag full of clothes left over from her kids. Many items were new and still had tags on them. As they were poured onto the floor, my kids descended on them like vultures.

I got a second job typing the newsletter for a local country club. It would have been wonderful to afford to be a member. This job brought in a thousand dollars a month, keeping my finances from going into the red. The kids would help me fold the letters and stuff them into envelopes. Then I would drop the envelopes off at the club, to be sent out to the members.

During this time I learned a lot about graphics, which I have since put to good use. Plus, my keyboarding skills significantly improved. Although my finances were tight, I don't think the children suffered or noticed. As long as they had a warm, clean home with food and clothes, they were happy.

\* \* \*

After being divorced for a few years from Dick, I decided to get married again. George, my new husband, was a friend of Dick's and mine, and we had been dating on and off for a couple of years. He moved in with me, bringing his two children with him.

George was very different from Dick. He was more even tempered and had a positive attitude. I thought I was in love with him at the time, but on reflecting back, I think I just wanted to share my life and the upbringing of my children with a healthy man. George seemed to be that man. In many ways he was my mentor as well as my friend.

One thing he had in common with Dick, which is a primary requirement for me in marrying a man, was his intelligence. Both men were very bright and augmented me in areas where I had things to learn. Having a mentor in the business world is so important. Mine just happened to be my husband.

George had just purchased his own small business and was cash tight, so we were very frugal. We were like a dysfunctional Brady Bunch, with six kids spread out over a six-year age range. Each child had their own issues and problems, some of them serious and others going hand in hand with adolescence. It was not an easy time for us to go through as parents. Little problems from the past got much bigger as the children became young adults.

> Having a mentor in the business world is so important.

\* \* \*

As time went on, working at Amalgamated Produce became more and more uncomfortable. Who works well with their estranged husband? Dick never wanted the divorce and was angry that I'd remarried. Deep down I understood. Both of us wanted me to leave, but I had no outside job experience for the previous ten years except teaching chemistry labs at various colleges part time.

Growing sprouts was a tedious job and not what I wanted to do for the rest of my life. It was hard work and produced a meager yield.

Yet I did recognize the value of all the experience I was gaining at Amalgamated Produce. I learned to deal with supermarkets, brokers, sell sheets, promotions, employee issues, operational and trucking issues, profit/loss calculations, spreadsheets, and many other challenges. Last but not least, I learned more about my talents and strengthened my desire to find my passion. I could feel it was around the corner someplace but not with Amalgamated Produce.

As my relationship with Dick became more and more strained, it was not an easy time for either of us. After seven years of operating the company together, a headhunter offered me a job as manager of customer service for a distribution company called Industrial Ingredients in Norwalk, Connecticut. Having no choice but to take the position, I started in June of 1996. Money was needed at home to help support the family, and Amalgamated was struggling.

\* \* \*

The job was an immediate disappointment, and I found myself teary-eyed more than once while driving to work. Industrial Ingredients was bleak and cold. The job title of manager was misleading since most of my work entailed entering purchase orders and arranging the transportation of goods. My expectations and capabilities surpassed the responsibilities of a customer service representative and order entry clerk. Periodically my boss, Fred, would give me a special project. However, most of the time, the job was repetitive.

As I was still a 50 percent owner of Amalgamated Produce, I would touch base daily. I counted the days till I could save up enough money to quit my job and buy or start my own company. During lunch breaks I would surf the internet, looking for business opportunities. I realized how much I enjoyed working for myself.

I was not used to a corporate job where people did not appear to work as a team. One time, for example, I suggested to the owner that we obtain domain rights for the name Industrial Ingredients and offered to apply for him. The next day Fred approached me, annoyed that I had gone directly to his boss, and told me to "stay in my lane." My purpose had been to help, not to be concerned with the protocol of going through Fred.

I was not used to that at Amalgamated Produce and was determined that sharing ideas would be encouraged if I were ever to start my own business. Industrial Ingredients employed about twenty office personnel, and I do not think any of them was happy. The culture was toxic to me. However, my stint at Industrial Ingredients did give me some valuable experience working in a company larger than Amalgamated Produce.

As it turned out after one year, they let me go due to restructuring. Perhaps they also realized I was not too fond of the job and was overqualified. Part of me felt rejected; after all who likes to be terminated by an employer? Yet I was so happy. On my drive home, I couldn't help but sing out loud, knowing that unemployment benefits were available for me while I looked for an opportunity to start a business.

\* \* \*

I immediately drove back to Amalgamated Produce and said to Dick, "I'm back. My position at Industrial Ingredients has been terminated."

His reaction? "Oh no. What happened? I don't want you here." He actually got teary-eyed with disappointment at seeing me.

In a way the scene was comical. But I understood that he wanted to run the business alone and did not want to pay me a salary again nor have a day-to-day relationship with an ex-wife. Yet he recognized that Amalgamated needed someone in sales and marketing. He also knew I owned half the business and didn't have a job. So we agreed that I would work part time in sales and marketing while looking for a new business for myself.

* * *

While working twenty hours a week for API, I pursued avenues to purchase or start my own company. If you want to be an entrepreneur, you keep plugging away, looking for that opportunity. I went through a business broker and considered purchasing a microfiche company. It was not difficult to see that microfiche would be going out with new technology coming in. Many people today don't even know what a microfiche is. That opportunity was quickly rejected.

Next, I found a small local advertising newspaper that featured local news stories and articles on topics such as decorating and travel. It was called *Home and Leisure*. One man owned the newspaper, and he wanted to move on to other things. It looked interesting. So for five thousand dollars, I bought the small operation. No assets came with the purchase, just the right to use the newspaper's name, but the price was affordable.

It did not take me long to realize that this newspaper business was not for me. Income was generated by going from business to business selling ads in the paper. Articles were obtained from the Associated Press or other sources. After I had secured the ads and articles, I would give everything to a graphic designer, and she would put the proofs together. Then we'd send the job to a printer, and from there the paper would be distributed for free to diners, stores, and restaurants. As customers were walking out the doors of these businesses, they would grab the paper and flip through it.

Selling advertisements to tiny businesses was hard for me. I felt like a door-to-door vacuum cleaner salesperson, and it reminded me of the old days of selling Avon. The business offered little growth opportunity. So I decided to close it down after just one cycle.

\* \* \*

In 1997 after rejoining API, I went into New York City to look for new customers to purchase either our sprouts or perhaps some of our less perishable items such as dried berries, wild rice, or homestyle dried bean soup mix. One of the customers was Gourmet Garage, a small, upscale gourmet food shop opening its third store in Manhattan. I arranged a meeting with the buyer a week before my visit. The day before my appointment, I confirmed the meeting to ensure that the buyer would be available.

As I walked in, he was on the phone, talking to a vendor, and turned to me, saying, "Who are you? What do you want with me? Notice I am very busy."

After I reminded him of our appointment, for which I had traveled a good part of the day and prepared a presentation, he said, "Oh, yeah. I don't have the time to see you, so leave the samples on the table. If I'm interested, I'll give you a call."

He was busy purchasing essential items such as meat and potatoes. The esoteric items I was offering were of low priority to him. I remember talking to Jean from the wall phone at Grand Central Station as I waited for my return train, complaining about the dismissive reception I'd gotten. Not only had I been ignored but the buyer also had been quite rude and used a few four-letter words on his phone call that were new to my vocabulary. Sales calls can be so disheartening.

About a week later, I received a phone call from one of the three owners of Gourmet Garage, telling me he saw my samples sitting on the table. He was not interested in the items I brought in. However, he was interested in something else.

He had seen our products in Costco and knew we were somewhat local and had production workers. He asked if we would be interested in packaging ninety types of food items, such as grains, granolas, dried fruit, nuts, trail mixes, and candy. The product needed to be packed in clear PET containers and private-labeled. He told me that his own people were currently labeling the product in their basement, but it was too time consuming. It was also difficult for the employees to maintain correct labeling and weights. Would Amalgamated be interested in taking over this task?

My answer: "Wow! Of course!"

\* \* \*

I immediately learned Microsoft Excel to price out the items requested. Dick worked with me to source all ninety products and helped secure the lowest cost possible. After a couple of months, the final price list was presented to Gourmet Garage. The original buyer who'd been so rude to me had left Gourmet Garage and had been replaced by Rob, which was a relief to me.

When I presented the pricing to Rob, his only question was, "When can you start?" He seemed delighted. I thought for sure he would discuss pricing, terms, and delivery. We were fair in our pricing, and I like to avoid haggling if possible. No haggling was needed. API started on the job the following week.

The day we delivered products to the stores, the employees at Gourmet Garage were so excited to see us. They no longer had to hand-pack these items in the basement and could now attend to doing what they were hired to do—manage their supermarket. We got a great reception and felt like a team.

This new business generated about three hundred thousand dollars in annual revenue to start. This was significant since sales from sprouts were only about $1.2 million a year. I recognized this as a great opportunity to either grow Amalgamated Produce or split off this aspect of the business into a separate entity. Maybe I'd finally found the opportunity I had been seeking all these years.

After talking with Dick, he agreed that I could form a new corporation and take Gourmet Garage as a customer in return for his owning some shares of the new company. It was the best decision for both of us. Packaging nuts and dried fruits in a humid environment would not be good for the product line. Besides, Dick wanted me out of Amalgamated Produce as much as I wanted to leave. We both wanted to lead our own separate lives.

Dick saw great opportunities down the road with broccoli sprouts coming on the market as a validated cancer-fighting food. Johns Hopkins Research Center had developed a patent for broccoli sprouts, proclaiming they carried a compound called sulforaphane. This natural chemical had a powerful ability to protect cells from the sort of damage that can instigate cancer. Dick was eager to obtain the rights from Johns Hopkins and to sell broccoli sprouts under their patent at Amalgamated Produce. He expected sales to increase significantly over the next few years from this new item.

Initially we both owned 50 percent of Amalgamated Produce and split the ownership of the new company, 60 percent belonging to me and 40 percent to Dick. A year later Dick wanted to buy me out of Amalgamated entirely so that he would own all of Amalgamated Produce. In return I would own all the new company's shares. Amalgamated was doing well with broccoli sprouts, and Dick was planning on expanding to mung beans and wheatgrass. His annual sales were growing and eventually reached over two and a half million dollars. I was just as excited as he was to sever ties. It was time.

Although Amalgamated Produce enjoyed some continuing good years, it eventually had a devastating recall due to listeria in 2009. The FDA started coming down seriously on sprout growers after several cases of illness were reported throughout the country. Dick decided to sell the company, being unable to recoup his losses. In retrospect I was lucky to leave when I did. Dick eventually sold the company, and it stayed in business for only a year before closing.

# AURORA
# PRODUCTS INC.

## *GETTING SET UP*

*Your work is going to fill a large part of your life, and the only*
*way to be truly satisfied is to do what you believe is great*
*work. And the only way to do great work is to love what you*
*do. If you haven't found it yet, keep looking. Don't settle.*

— STEVE JOBS

Before incorporating the new company, a name had to be chosen. Amalgamated Products agreed to rent a thousand square feet to the developing company for a short period, and we would share the secretary. So realizing that the only office employee we had, Jean, was answering the phone with "Hello, this is API. How can I help you?" we decided the new company should have the same acronym. It would be strange if Jean said, "Hello. API and Stephanie's Nuts."

I went through the dictionary, looking up proper names that started with an *A. Hmmm, Aurora sounds nice.* So that was what we settled on. The *P* and *I* were easier. Aurora Products Inc. now had the same initials as Amalgamated Produce Inc. and was ready to be incorporated. Now when Jean answered the phone, she could say, "Hello? API. How can I help you?" and represent both companies.

I asked a young attorney friend of mine to incorporate the company. I don't know how much confidence he had in Aurora's success, because he gave me my corporate papers in a cheap three-ring binder. Maybe he didn't think it would last too long. In any case we were officially in business. Eventually the corporate book was replaced with a leather-bound book and an official stamp for Aurora Products.

Aurora Products developed from perseverance and luck—perseverance in looking for business ideas and luck in finding the opportunity. As stated earlier Amalgamated Produce was no longer challenging or fun for me. I was forty-six years old now and remarried, and our children were more independent. My second husband and I were able to help each other financially. It was a perfect situation for starting a business. Timing is important. Many people seek opportunities to start a business and trip over them without looking down. I was fortunate to recognize the right opportunity at the right time.

\* \* \*

In the beginning the new company had four employees. I felt like a one-armed paperhanger, taking on the roles of salesperson, order entry clerk, bookkeeper, and packer. Our equipment consisted of a pile of pallets with a piece of plywood on top to form a table. After placing a vinyl tablecloth on top of the stacked pallets and adding a postal scale, we were in business. George built a lockable storage room for our bulk product after realizing that several of the Amalgamated employees were helping themselves to the nuts and candies we were packing a hundred feet away from them.

Today our initial setup at Amalgamated's facility would not pass muster with third-party audits, visits from the FDA, and organic and kosher certification requirements. If auditors had seen our small operation, I am sure they would indeed have shut us down. Regulations require steel or vinyl-covered tables, professional scales, and a clean, dry environment for packing food. Makeshift tables from stacked pallets would have resulted in the immediate cancellation of our food license. The neighborhood also had mice and rats. The humidity was high due to the drums of hydroponically grown sprouts within the building, and we offered no formal education on sanitation.

However, as I said, it was a different time, and we were learning. Also, we somewhat slipped under the wire for any agency to know we existed. Realistically we knew we could not stay in the Amalgamated facility long term. It was not a good environment for storing or packaging our items.

\* \* \*

My first employee was Elba. She was a thirty-six-year-old Hispanic woman with a broad smile. She and her fifty-six-year-old husband supported their four children in Bridgeport in a home they purchased through Habitat for Humanity. Habitat for Humanity helps people who have jobs and a desire to purchase a home but need a leg up. The charity purchases houses and fixes them up with help from volunteers and the family. In the end the family gets a home and an affordable mortgage. Times were tough for Elba's family, and they barely made minimum wage. I remember offering Elba the supervisor position after recognizing her strong work ethic at Amalgamated, and Dick agreed to let her come with me.

Elba accepted the offer with an ear-to-ear grin. As she was leaving the lunchroom afterward, she jumped up to tap the top of the door. I'll never forget that happy jump. The promotion gave her hope in providing more income for her family and purpose in helping form a new company. She immediately went out and found four of her favorite workers, people she could depend on, to help push products out the door. They were all hard workers.

To this day, twenty-two years later, Elba is still an Aurora employee and has been promoted up the ranks over the years. She is well respected and proud to be introduced to visitors as one of the original employees. I beam with pride right beside her. She and I have come a long way together.

* * *

There was a lot of excitement about this new company and its aspirations for success. Some of the people working at Amalgamated asked to be relocated to the back room, where they were packing nuts and the environment was drier—not understanding that Aurora was a separate outfit. Dick was not too pleased and told them to stay where they were and to continue packing sprouts.

At first Aurora worked hard at satisfying our one and only customer, Gourmet Garage. We private-labeled their items, including nuts, dried fruits, candies, grains, granolas, and trail mixes. Initially they had three stores and eventually, at their height, owned six stores. Years later they sold out to ShopRite since it was hard to compete with Whole Foods in the city. During those first eighteen years, Aurora owed a lot of gratitude to Gourmet Garage for the opportunity to start our business.

After building up some confidence and experience in what we had to offer, I went into New York, pounding the pavement to drum up new customers and build the business. I thought that if Gourmet Garage liked the way Aurora packaged their items with their private label, other specialty markets might like it too. I was right. Most stores in New York City were packaging their nuts and sticking deli labels on them. An attractive label with the store's private logo was much more enticing and professional.

After a year I realized I needed help in sales and hired a friend, Jan, to take on the sales role. For the next couple of years, we aggressively focused on building up business by selling privately labeled items to stores. Jan worked part time yet managed to bring in quite a few customers from New York City and Westchester County. It was not difficult for her since Aurora was one of the frontrunners in the world of private-label snacks. We had the advantage of getting many accounts before competitive companies spotted our idea and entered the market.

* * *

In addition to small markets, Aurora also sought larger stores and alternative markets such as Bed Bath & Beyond, Burlington, and others. Bed Bath & Beyond showed interest in carrying some of our candies and nuts in their five-hundred-plus stores in the 1980s. At one time they had over a thousand stores. Today I believe their storefronts are closing down due to changes in the economy and the purchasing habits of consumers.

Servicing a primary account was a great opportunity for us, and Bed Bath & Beyond became our largest customer. However, they were challenging to deal with, and delivery was costly. At that time, they wanted delivery to be made through UPS to each of their stores. If there was a shortage or a damaged shipment, each store would submit a separate deduction sheet. When we received payment, each store's invoices and deductions were listed. Reconciling it all cost us hours of labor.

After we'd been doing business with Bed Bath & Beyond for a couple of years, the buyer informed us they found meal moths in our pistachios. An embarrassing lull in the conversation ensued, and we agreed to have the items sent back to Aurora. That was a mistake. Not only did we have to reimburse them for the item at retail cost (as opposed to the price they paid for it) but we were also billed the freight for the return of the product. To make matters worse, no meal moths were found in the product. Some of the pistachio containers were not even ours. This incident cost us tens of thousands of dollars, money we could ill afford to lose.

> Sometimes when you have a big fish, you need to make sure the costs and setbacks of hauling it in do not eat up all the meat and leave you with just bones.

After much consideration we decided that doing business with Bed Bath & Beyond was costing us too much in fees and shipping. We were not making a profit. It was a difficult decision since their sales made up 30 percent of our revenue. Yet we discontinued them as a customer. Sometimes when you have a big fish, you need to make sure the costs and setbacks of hauling it in do not eat up all the meat and leave you with just bones.

* * *

Initially all I had was $110,000 from the sale of Amalgamated Products to Dick (and some credit cards) to fund the business. That may sound like a lot of money, but it goes quickly when you need to purchase equipment and inventory and fund labor costs. Over the next few years, there were additional funds from Amalgamated's sale, but those were earmarked for paying my four children's college education. Money was tight.

Often George would lend me a few thousand dollars. He happened to start his own advertising business, totally unrelated to Aurora, at around the same time, and we would act as each other's bank when one of us needed to float some ready cash. It was a fun time for George and me to watch each other's business grow. Why I was not scared or fearful of failure, I don't know. After all, defeat would be difficult to accept, considering the six children were still in school and some were attending college. I guess being pumped up with adrenaline and passion didn't leave room for failure.

George was a big help to me in setting up Aurora. He had experience working in sales and marketing at Bristol Myers and Combe Inc., a personal hygiene company in White Plains, New York. Often George would accompany me to auctions to help me pick up used office equipment, forklifts, racks, pallet jacks, carts, scales, used vans, and other necessary items. Most of the time, he was helpful. Sometimes his enthusiasm got the better of him.

One time we went to an auction that was selling forklifts. My limit for a forklift was four thousand dollars. Bidding started at a thousand dollars, but someone kept betting against me. It was not until a few bids went back and forth that I saw George standing at the other end of the row, holding his number high in the air. He was trying to purchase the machine for me, not realizing we were bidding against each other. After that we always stood together when going to auctions. Now most auctions take place online, which is not as fun. I enjoyed the excitement of the live affair and miss it now.

One time George and I went to an auction for a company liquidating its equipment and going bankrupt. The building was on Long Beach Boulevard in Stratford, and it had high ceilings, ample parking, and loading docks. We purchased some pallet racking and some miscellaneous equipment at the auction. As we left the building, I remarked to George, "Someday I hope Aurora will be big enough to afford a building as big and impressive as this one." I had high aspirations for our growth as we continued to purchase new equipment to accommodate our needs.

In the beginning we bought most of our production equipment and office furniture secondhand or at auctions. I am still using the secondhand desk I purchased from George's friend selling off his office furniture. After a while we bought some new equipment and a brand-new forklift.

# SORTING OUT INSURANCE NEEDS

*You can't run a business without taking risks.*

−ERNST ZUNDEL

G etting set up for insurance coverage for Aurora was fairly straightforward. I used the same agent who represented us at Amalgamated. There are numerous coverages you need, including building insurance, commercial liability, workers' compensation, keyman insurance, employee practices, terrorism, commercial auto, and business interruption. Have I forgotten anything? The list goes on. Then there are additional lines you may need for your specific business. My third and present husband, Steve, recently related a story that illustrates the hidden landmines you can encounter when buying insurance.

Years ago he owned a company that rented canoes and rafts to people looking for a fun ride down the Housatonic River. He would drive them up the river with their canoe that they rented for the day and drop them off. It would take a few hours for them to canoe back down the river, return the canoes, and go to their cars. Although the river was usually calm, there were times of the year when the water rushed and the boats encountered some rapids. Concerned about potential exposure, Steve got insurance from his agent.

A year later while looking through the policy, he noticed that the insurance was for the business and building only and excluded any accidents due to water. He was dumbfounded that the agent had never mentioned this and didn't understand Steve's most significant liability—somebody getting hurt while in one of his canoes. The lesson here is that you must look after yourself to ensure all bases are covered. Never depend totally on your agent to advise you of all coverages you have and don't have. Don't find out you lack a specific coverage only when the time arrives that you need it. Luckily Steve never encountered trouble on the river.

> **You must look after yourself to ensure all bases are covered.**

* * *

One of the coverages I didn't have initially was product recall insurance. I didn't know it existed. It never dawned on me that if I were to have a recall costing hundreds of thousands of dollars and my standard policy did not cover it, I would be responsible for the debt. I thought I had coverage.

One day we received a call from the FDA. One of the labels for our trail mix did not have "contains sulfites" printed on the nutritional panel. Someone from the FDA spotted it at a store and forced us to have a recall. At that time our sales were small, so not much volume was involved. Yet we were all over the news on TV and in newspapers. The local anchorman announced, "There is a nationwide recall on Aurora

Products' dried apricots due to failure to label the presence of sulfites, a known allergen." They reported that we sold containerloads of the stuff.

This was my first introduction to fake news. We sold about a hundred cases of the product to three small stores, not a hundred containerloads nationwide. I wish I had contacted our insurance agent to discuss recall coverage at that time. However, since the total cost of recalling the product, plus fees, was not too high for Aurora, we resolved the issue without the insurance company's knowledge.

Had the recall been revealed to my broker, he would have told us we didn't have adequate coverage, and we would have added recall insurance to our policy for future protection. Unfortunately when we had a later, larger recall due to an issue with Peanut Corporation, we didn't have coverage. And that recall turned out to be *very* expensive.

\* \* \*

We bought raw peanuts from Peanut Corporation wholesale, repacked them, and sold them to supermarkets. I informed our agent that we had a recall issue due to the FDA's finding salmonella contamination in peanuts from Peanut Corporation. As a result we had to pull our items off supermarket shelves. He told us we didn't have recall insurance and that this was a unique type of coverage. It was an expensive lesson and cost Aurora over three hundred thousand dollars in fees and returned product. Since then, we've made sure we have recall insurance. A recall can put you out of business or set you back significantly if you do not have coverage.

I would love to say we've only had one or two recalls, but recalls are a constant threat that we work hard at avoiding. The danger comes with the business, akin to souring being milk's biggest nemesis. Our latest recall resulted from purchasing chocolate from a reputable company that did not declare milk on its ingredient panel. This mistake was passed down to us and many other repackers and distributors of the chocolate. So when I say the *R* word is something we cringe at, I mean it.

Occasionally Rick will come into my office from quality control, saying, "Stephanie, we have a problem."

My heart jumps into my throat as I say hesitantly, "Does it start with an *R*?"

"No," he'll reply, and my blood pressure will return to normal.

* * *

An aspect of insurance that can be challenging is workers' compensation. The purpose of this insurance is to pay for injuries to people that occur while on the job. Yet employees, as well as health providers, often take advantage of this insurance. For example, I had one worker, Harry, come into work after a long weekend. He was sitting in the lunchroom, holding his swollen knee, blurting out how he'd hurt it playing street ball with his nephew over the weekend. "Man! I blew out my knee when I fell on the asphalt!"

He worked through the day but called out sick the following day, saying his knee hurt him and needed medical care. The claim? Yup, he damaged it at work. So he got time off to recuperate, physical therapy, and other medical attention. This annoys me, as we can do nothing about it except stress safety at work.

We had another employee who had several different operations on various parts of her body and claimed they should fall under workers' compensation. She had both wrists operated on for carpal tunnel syndrome, shoulder surgery, and knee surgery, and then her back was bothering her. Nobody wanted to say these problems were due to her arthritis. Behind the scenes she earned the nickname Bionic Woman due to her multiple implants.

# EXPANSION INTO NEW LOCATIONS

*God prunes us when He is about to take us into*
*a new season of growth and expansion.*

—CHRISTINE CAINE

After one year of operating in the thousand-square-foot space at Amalgamated Produce, Aurora concluded that the building was too small to handle our business. In addition, humidity from the hydroponic growing of sprouts was not good for the nuts, which required a cool environment with low humidity. After much looking around in Bridgeport, we found a nine-thousand-square-foot building on Island Brook Avenue. My budget was low, so we had to compromise by selecting a building without a loading dock. This meant that when deliveries were made or trucks loaded, we would have to handload everything from the high truck to the ground or vice versa. Eventually I purchased a saddle stacker, which would be manually pushed to the vehicle, and the forks or tines would lift the pallet. Motorized forklifts were too expensive at the time.

The building was made of brick and had been used as a garage or auto shop. I called the Connecticut Health Department and Department of Agriculture to help guide us in retrofitting the building up to code. The first thing required was to get new flooring. Painting the old floor with hard, gray epoxy paint was the solution agreed upon, so I started immediately. I hired Elba's son to help, but teenage boys worked too slowly for me. I put on my old pants, wrapped my feet in black garbage bags to protect my shoes, and painted away. In one week we were finished. The walls were sprayed with clear water-repellant solution, sinks were installed in the warehouse, and overhead lights were covered with plastic to protect people from exploding glass should the light bulbs break. After three weeks we moved into our new home.

About four months into our stay at the new facility, we began to periodically hear the scurrying of little feet behind pallets before turning on the lights in the early morning hours. It turned out we had mice. I hated to poison them, and I also knew it would be hazardous to use poison in a food establishment. Another alternative was to use traps or glue boards. If you have ever seen a mouse attached to a glue board with its face half torn off, you would agree it is a gruesome sight. So that was not an option for me. In discussing our mouse problem with a coworker, she said her husband's company had a litter of kittens outside near their dumpster. Hmm. My mind was ticking, and I thought it would be an excellent idea for Aurora to get a cat. I didn't consider what the health department or any regulatory agencies would think about this.

We called our new member, Amber, because she was a beautiful calico with amber coloring mixed with her brown and white fur. She was sweet, but her dietary choices did not include mice. Amber was not a hunter—in fact, she was afraid of mice—and preferred eating peanut butter sandwiches that employees carelessly left on the lunch table. After a while Amber came home with me and became a house cat. Maybe it was fate's way of teaching me that having animals in a food production plant was a big no-no. I was naive at the time and had so much to learn.

* * *

Unbeknownst to me when the lease was signed in late 1998, the river beside our building had poor drainage and was prone to flooding. In addition, the plumbing was ancient; and when it rained, the rainwater from the roof went into the same drain as the sewage. The landlord knew this but, in his eagerness to rent the facility, failed to mention this little problem. He was a macho man who called women "goils" and made overtly sexist remarks, such as claiming his wife didn't mind his "indiscretions" with other women as long as she didn't know about them.

Several times after a heavy rain, water from the roof would pour into the sewage drain and erupt like the geyser at Yellowstone National Park from an open pipe next to the front door. The major difference was that it was not fresh water but rather murky water containing human waste and feminine products. It was disgusting. The landlord would come by, grumble, and blame it on the "goils" flushing their personal items, and an argument would eventually ensue. Of course, we would immediately clean up the mess and sanitize the area, but every time it rained, I was nervous.

One Saturday in 2001, I had gotten my hair permed in preparation for a formal function that evening. As I left the beauty parlor, it started to pour rain outside. My immediate thought was the possibility of Aurora flooding. I sped to the facility, and sure enough there were about four inches of water in the production area. We had several pallets of expensive nuts and grains on the floor, and I panicked. I immediately called Elba, as well as my husband and our buyer, Jeff, to help me vacuum up the water and sweep it outside as the flash flood continued.

After working and sweating for about three hours and after the rain subsided, we managed to get rid of the water. I went into the bathroom to wash my hands and looked in the mirror. Yeow! Looking back at me through the glass was a bedraggled woman with the hairdo of Frankenstein's wife. There was no way my hair could be tamed in time for the function that night. The only party I'd be allowed to attend would be a Halloween party.

After this frantic day, we all realized that Aurora had to get out of that location if we did not want the health department to close us down. The landlord was of no help and said the situation was beyond his control. We immediately started looking for a new facility to house our plant, not only because of the water issue but also because our business was growing quickly, and we needed more space.

Sales were growing as we acquired more customers. In addition, Gourmet Garage opened a couple of more stores, which substantially increased our orders. I recall Elba working very hard and often putting in overtime. Whenever an order would come in, she would fulfill it right away, never letting me down. Sometimes a customer would submit an order late in the afternoon, just as Elba's crew was finishing up for the day. I would hand the order to her, knowing she would be upset at the last-minute order. She would flail her arms around, expressing how late it was and how difficult it would be for people to stay. Then with a wry smile, she would look at me and say, "No problem, we'll get it done. I'll talk to my crew."

* * *

In 2001 we found some land in Bridgeport on Mountain Grove Avenue—which we were assured was in an area not susceptible to flooding—and we built a thirteen-thousand-square-foot facility as our new home. It was a challenge for me to construct a building from scratch, but I felt I had no choice. I needed a building with a loading dock, high ceilings, a food-grade environment, and a decent location in Bridgeport where I would not get mugged. There was nothing available that met our criteria.

I had a great contractor who basically did everything, so my challenge became easier. At the very end, when everything was done, the contractor poured a bit of cement at the corner of the building where my children were able to put their handprints. Maybe in fifty years, if the building is still there, they can go back and reminisce about that busy time in our lives.

Everyone at Aurora was excited and had developed a strong camaraderie. I knew the names of all forty employees and much about their family lives. Not having encountered a great variety of ethnic groups in my sheltered youth in the country, I was thrilled to be invited to Hispanic weddings, African American inner-city church sermons, pig roasts, funerals, and baby showers. I hired a private tutor, Edda, to teach my husband and me Spanish at home. (One of my biggest mistakes in school was having learned French instead of Spanish.) Edda also helped employees at Aurora learn English. Every Wednesday she would work with anyone who wanted to learn. The office manager would announce, "La maestra Edda está aquí. Todos los empleados que estén interesados, por favor venir a la oficina para su clase semanal de inglés." In English this means "The teacher Edda is here. All interested employees, please come to the office for your weekly English lesson."

When we moved into our new digs in 2002, I marveled at our spacious production area, storeroom, and office space. The building was brand new and clean and featured not only an overhead door but a much-needed loading dock as well. What a luxury! We no longer needed razor-wire fencing since the real estate was in a safe area of Bridgeport. I was proud of owning a growing business and constructing a Butler-style building that offered lots of space. That changed quickly—space became tighter as we continued to grow.

In 2003 we were growing so fast that we needed to purchase additional equipment and hire new people. We also decided to become more automated. That was when we bought our first "cow." This was an automatic filling line that labeled and tamperproofed the containers. We called it the cow because its hydraulic mechanism sounded like a cow mooing. The name has stuck with us, and now we have more than ten cows.

In 2005, three years after moving to Mountain Grove Avenue, we needed to move again, because we felt like sardines packed in a can. It was incredible how quickly we filled up the space. I never thought we would outgrow the facility so quickly.

\* \* \*

We wanted to stay in Bridgeport, which allowed easy access to labor and was close to my home. But there were no buildings in Bridgeport that offered us what we needed. The next town over, Stratford, had an industrial park with available space. So our real estate broker took me in his car to look at the warehouse buildings.

You can imagine the look on my face when I saw that one of the available buildings was at 350 Long Beach Boulevard. This was the exact building I had visited during one of the auctions with George— the one I hoped Aurora could someday afford. We were there. We rented the space immediately.

The space was initially thirty-nine thousand square feet. After the first year, we needed more room for additional offices and the employee lunchroom, so we took on another six thousand square feet. We were again out of space a year later, and our landlord offered us space across the parking lot. Twice more, we added footage. We kept expanding until we were renting about seventy-five thousand square feet.

When the landlord could no longer offer us extra space at what we considered a fair rental price, we finally decided to purchase a building with some extra land around it for future growth. In 2011 we found a place in Orange, Connecticut. It was a ninety-five-thousand-square-foot building that previously housed a gem refining and sorting company. It was located on thirteen and a half acres of land, which offered us plenty of growth possibilities. It had a large safe inside that had to be removed, which was probably why we were able to purchase the building for $2.5 million. I kept hoping that maybe I would step on a diamond or ruby that had gotten lost in the rubble, but no such luck. Of course, we spent another seven million to renovate the facility, but when it was finished, it was perfect.

The flow of production was designed so that when a product arrived in the receiving area, it went directly to the cooler instead of being pushed across the whole production floor as in some of our other buildings. The flow of processing is essential, as it affects production time. In 2012 we moved in.

**The flow of processing is essential, as it affects production time.**

We have continued to add more space. As of this writing, we're at a hundred forty thousand square feet and plan to add twenty thousand more. We have added a large refrigerator and freezer, which helps keep our product fresh. I walk around the building and am so proud of my staff, production workers, and friends. The neighborhood is more rural, so employees can enjoy grass and trees, yet it is located close to I-95.

# FINDING
# YOUR TEAM

*Great things in business are never done by one
person. They're done by a team of people.*

— STEVE JOBS

tarting up a corporation with limited funds doesn't make
it easy to find experienced candidates for employment
positions. So in our early days, instead of looking at
education and experience, we would look at candidates'
potential and work ethics. As mentioned earlier Elba was one such
person who had work ethics and intellect. She knew how to prioritize
orders and get things done.

Today she continues to work at Aurora. She has gotten older
now, with short, gray, cropped hair, and her children have all left the
nest. She and her husband moved out of Bridgeport and now live in
a one-floor condo within five miles of Aurora, allowing Miguel, her
husband, easier access to the bedroom as he ages. We have shared

stories and problems with our children over the years and given each other advice and consolation when needed.

In the early years of Aurora's development, her husband made wooden racks by hand for some retail stores that wanted to carry our products. He had a woodworking shop in his basement to help augment the family's income. Today he is over eighty-two years old and no longer helps us, but his contributions throughout the years have been invaluable. Many of our racks in stores still bear his stamp.

Art, a driver we had for over twelve years, no longer works for Aurora due to his retirement, yet he was a loyal employee I could always count on. I respected him because he worked two jobs to put his grandson through Notre Dame High School, a private school in Bridgeport. Family was everything to him, and he took good care of them. He was about five foot seven and usually sported a two-day shadow of a beard, an unlit cigar in his teeth, and a tummy hanging over his belt. Brad Pitt he was not, but he protected the interests of Aurora and never let us down. He was one of those people who loved to hug me and call me sweetie. Under most circumstances calling the CEO of Aurora sweetie is not allowed. Most employees call me Stephanie or in some cases, out of respect, Ms. Stephanie. However, Art came aboard when we were very small and somehow got away with it from day one.

> **Successful people recognize the strengths and talents of others and provide them the platform to forge ahead.**

Successful people recognize the strengths and talents of others and provide them the platform to forge ahead. The success of the individual contributes to corporate success and vice versa. Several people in the office are in their positions because they excel at what they do, and I feel proud to know I helped put them there.

\* \* \*

About a year after starting Aurora, while talking to Rob, the buyer at Gourmet Garage, I asked him if he knew anybody with his enthusiasm and quick mind. He was in his mid-thirties, curious, and always open to new ideas. Aurora could not hire him since he was our best customer's lead buyer, but I asked him if maybe he could point me in the right direction to find his clone. He cocked his head and said with a wry smile, "Clones are inferior to the original being, but I can do one better. I have an identical twin brother, Jeff, who is looking for a job. Maybe he can come in for an interview?"

Wow, an identical twin brother! Jeff was promptly invited to Aurora for an interview. He came to visit us in a suit and tie. It was one of the few times I have seen him dressed like that. As we spoke I felt like I was talking to Rob.

As a contrast to Jeff's formality, my sky-blue parakeet, Polly, had gotten out of his cage and was flying around the room. I had rescued Polly from my son, who was off to college, and he came to work with me every day. Polly decided, for some reason, to test Jeff's patience. As Jeff strove to behave professionally, Polly paced back and forth on the desk and eventually landed on his shoulder. He looked up at Jeff's nervously darting eyes, chirping at him as if to coach him through his interview. I could barely maintain a straight face. Jeff was too apprehensive to say anything, probably realizing that the woman interviewing him was a tad eccentric. He just quietly brushed Polly off his shoulder, and the bird flew back to his cage. Jeff said nothing. One month later Jeff was hired and has remained with us ever since. We still chuckle over his first interview with me and Polly.

When Polly later flew away one day, Jeff didn't seem too disappointed. Yet realizing I liked animals and allowed them in the office, he went out and bought his own animals, two water frogs named Matt and Greg, after my two sons. They lived for quite a few years in his aquarium at work.

Jeff has been a great asset to Aurora. When he came on board, he knew very little about nuts. Now he is an expert and has helped Aurora secure large contracts with farms worldwide. His buying skills are top notch, and Aurora was lucky to find him.

* * *

Candy is one of my favorite employees and mentees. She came to Aurora from the Dominican Republic as a young teenage girl with thick black hair, flashy clothes, lots of curves, and a sassy attitude. Her mother joined Aurora as an unskilled packer, and Candy would often join her when we needed workers. Candy had ambition and brains and saw Aurora as a place to grow. Her enthusiasm and problem-solving abilities were rare to find, so she was invited to work in the office instead of the factory.

She thrived and helped Aurora immensely. Candy immediately changed her wardrobe to reflect success and maturity. She now has a husband and two little girls. In appreciation for her contributions, Aurora has funded her college education with a few courses a year and will continue to do so until she gets her bachelor's degree, which lies right around the corner.

Candy promises me that she will stay at Aurora until I retire. At that time, she and her family plan on moving to Florida. Little does she know that retirement is not on my agenda until I'm well into my nineties. I plan to keep coming to the office even if it's in a wheelchair, dragging an oxygen tank. By the time I retire, Candy may be in a wheelchair herself. I don't want her to leave—she is not only my mentee but in many ways also my mentor.

Many other memorable people were hired in our first few years. Diana, for instance, started as a young thirty-four-year-old, attractive Hispanic woman with one son. She lived in a relatively poor area of Bridgeport and did everything for her son, including getting him a full scholarship to a private school. She has proved invaluable to Aurora with her mental sharpness, multitasking ability, and enthusiasm for the business. She's also one of the only people I know who have a perfectly straight set of white teeth without ever going to an orthodontist. Her smile takes over her whole face, a bit like Julia Roberts. She is still with Aurora and going strong. Since starting at Aurora, she's had three additional babies and juggles motherhood with being director of customer services. Nothing gets past Diana. Her passion for her children and Aurora is what drives her.

Rick joined Aurora as a fiftyish-year-old man. He has white hair, beautiful blue eyes, and a quick smile. He's also quick to grumble when something goes wrong. His first desk was in a small cubicle in the office due to our lack of space. To concentrate he would wear headphones to drown out the ambient noise. He now has his own office and staff. Rick is quite meticulous, but that is his job. After all he is the director of quality assurance and must abide by all laws. Safe, high-quality food is our number one priority. It takes constant attention and perseverance.

Sales are often thwarted by quality assurance paperwork, yet maintaining high standards keeps us at the top of our industry for quality and integrity. Rick has been with us now for over twelve years and is invaluable. I credit him and his staff for lifting us to new heights and helping Aurora earn the highest quality control certifications obtainable. We achieved a 98 percent score from a third-party audit for Safe Quality Food (SQF). That puts us in the top 5 percent for SQF, which is a challenging score to obtain. Very few of our competitors have received such a level.

# MAINTAINING HIGH-QUALITY FOODS

*Quality is not an act; it is a habit.*

–ARISTOTLE

aintaining the level of quality control achieved by Aurora is not easy and can sometimes be challenging, especially when unexpected things come up. Years ago, when we had a third-party audit of our facility in Stratford, the inspector walked around our facility, examining all surfaces, equipment, paperwork, food, and processes. He was also looking at pest control.

As you may know, birds can carry salmonella. When in flight or just perched, they leave their droppings everywhere and are taboo in a food-processing area. Yet it is impossible to guarantee that a bird or two will not fly under the loading dock doors. We try to lure stray birds out of the facility as quickly as possible to prevent them from flying over the food. In addition, we do everything we can to deter them from flying in by placing plastic strips at all dock entrances and wiring at the tops of doors. Sometimes they still manage to get in.

In this one case, the inspector was busily attending to his inspection when, lo and behold, a bird flew behind his head. Luckily he did not see it. We did everything we could to avert his eyes from the vagrant bird. Every time he turned his head toward the beam where the bird was perched, someone would deflect his attention. Eventually we steered him away from the area and blockaded the site until we could get rid of our pesky friend. It was comical yet potentially quite serious. We all sighed a breath of relief when we got rid of the bird without the inspector ever knowing.

Another pest we constantly battle in our arena is the meal moth. The four stages of the meal moth's life include the egg, larva (worm), pupa (cocoon), and adult. Life cycles range from 27 days to 305, depending on the environment. If the egg is inside a nice, warm building with nuts, it is closer to 27 days. If outside or in a cooler environment, it can take longer. These moths are indigenous to areas that grow grain and corn and can be found in many domestic kitchens. To prevent them at the company, we put up pheromone traps throughout the facility to lure the males. If we see any moths stuck to the sticky card inside the trap, we do a thorough search to ensure we don't have a pallet that has been infected.

If an infected pallet is found, we quarantine it to prevent further infestation and either immediately roast the nuts, which kills the infestation, or stick the product in the freezer for a month, which kills all growth stages of the moth. Unlike some other food-processing plants that are not all-natural, we cannot fumigate our storage rooms, as the chemicals may come in contact with the nuts and other foodstuffs.

Mice can sometimes find a way into our building, so we have a pest control company that checks weekly. We've painted white strips along all walls to enable us to see their droppings more easily, and we pull all pallet racking at least ten inches away from the walls to allow visibility and to eliminate a snug place for the four-legged critters to hide. Unlike earlier locations we inhabited, this facility is not a haven for rodents that wish to live a long life. We have traps all over and have blocked all entry holes. We should put up a small Beware sign to warn mice that Aurora Products is not a cozy place to hang out.

\* \* \*

Rick and his quality control team have helped enact aggressive cleaning practices that have prompted accolades from our FDA inspector. Other certifications include USDA Organic, Non-GMO Project Verified, Xerces Society's Bee Better certification, and kosher certification.

Once a year the organic inspector comes to our facility to validate our record keeping and verify that our organic suppliers are certified. The inspector also goes into our storage rooms to look at bulk products and peruse the accompanying paperwork so that we may maintain our "organic" seal. In the past it was easy for vendors to declare an item organic yet cheat on paperwork and sourcing. Now it isn't easy to forge paperwork since record keeping and tracking are mandated and linked. Our enterprise resource planning (ERP) system tracks and integrates all items, lots, and specifications within our main business processes.

In addition to the organic inspector's annual visit, our rabbi comes monthly. He looks at the product and asks if we have added any new items to his approval list for kosher. He's a pleasant man who sometimes brings his son or daughter with him to see a nut-packing company. I am not Jewish, but I have learned many Jewish customs throughout the years. One awkward mistake I once made was welcoming the rabbi with a spontaneous hug and handshake. He was taken aback and explained that, in his faith, he doesn't feel comfortable shaking hands, much less receiving hugs, from a woman. Now when he leaves, I give him the thumbs-up farewell.

Aurora has established sustainable environmental practices. We use postconsumer rPET packaging that is also 100 percent recyclable after use. The plastic is superior at keeping oxygen out and preserving product freshness. The company also struck a partnership with Newport Biodiesel to deliver twenty thousand pounds of used cooking oil from our roasters to be made into clean-burning biodiesel fuel. This reduces the amount of petroleum Connecticut needs to import. Aurora's manufacturing team works with utility companies and closes its plant for a few hours during peak utility usage times to conserve electric usage.

\* \* \*

In the production area, Aurora's internal food inspectors are constantly walking around the factory, inspecting the quality of the product. They look for inaccurate weights, contamination from foreign items, and errors in paperwork while also checking the quality of the product. This is important. A few years back, a supermarket found a frog packed in a bag of precut lettuce. I don't think it was still alive, but I envision it hopping around in there.

**They look for inaccurate weights, contamination from foreign items, and errors in paperwork while also checking the quality of the product.**

As explained earlier when discussing Amalgamated Produce, every food-processing company has critical control points. At Aurora we have three. One of them is correct, accurate labeling. We need to make sure all our retail packages are labeled adequately and contain all legal information such as allergen reporting.

A second critical control point is temperature and time roasting our nuts and peanuts (which are not actually nuts). Nuts and peanuts are grown outside under the elements where bacteria can proliferate. So to kill off the bacteria and make the product safe, Aurora roasts nuts under a controlled system. The nuts are roasted at a pre-validated temperature for a predetermined time frame that meets the criteria that have been established.

Our third critical control is the pasteurization process. Our process pasteurizes nuts and seeds with an organic-certified, plant-derived liquid that kills bacteria on the nuts. We use this system for raw nuts only since roasted nuts already include a kill.

Although not a critical control point, Aurora has also developed a protocol for metal detection. As a young child, I once found a dime in a Mary Jane candy. I was so excited. Not only did I get a chewy peanut butter candy but I also got a dime as a bonus. The story is nice, but if it had been a tack or a screw instead, I would not have been so happy. Since nuts are processed through automated equipment either at Aurora or the processing plant, it's possible for a piece of metal to drop into the product somewhere in the process. In some instances we have found buckshot and bullet shards in almonds from hunters shooting at birds sitting in almond trees. In addition, a screw or another piece of metal could fall into the product during harvesting or production. So our protocol is to pass our finished goods through a metal detector.

Another problem we work hard at avoiding at Aurora is under-weighing products by mistake. Years ago a popular and successful specialty market, Stew Leonard's, got into trouble for underweighing their products. I am not sure if they did it on purpose or by accident. Either way the FDA did not like it and acted to protect consumers by levying hefty fines on Stew Leonard's. This was followed by bad publicity. It was a "mistake" they will never make again. So at Aurora our quality control technicians routinely walk around the plant to double-check weights.

# FINDING A
# NEW SALES TEAM

*The strength of the team is each individual member.*
*The strength of each member is the team.*

**—PHIL JACKSON**

I n 2002, after being in business for four years, George asked me about my goals for Aurora. I had not thought that far ahead. Aurora was young, and I was enjoying watching sales grow and working with my people. Being skeptical I felt projections were a waste of time. For me the future was hard to conceptualize for Aurora.

After I expressed my lack of direction, George responded that I needed to make up my mind about whether I wanted to remain a mom-and-pop company selling private-labeled snacks to local stores or grow nationwide with my brand. I was not used to writing up business plans. At the end of each year, I would hastily put together an outline of things I wanted to pursue, but it was cryptic at best. No finances were mentioned, and it did not include board decisions or projections. We did not have a board to speak of. It consisted of one person, such as my son or daughter, and me. Once a year, board meetings took place over email and lasted about five minutes.

I liked the second option of growing nationwide and building a brand throughout the United States. So I designed a logo and package for the Aurora brand and planned on promoting it. I spent a lot of time under the hot spray of my morning shower thinking over and over what direction I wanted to go and how to develop my brand. Most of my creative thinking was done under that hot shower. One thing I knew was that I needed to try to land some significant customers instead of just small, independent stores. Second, I wanted to push the Aurora brand instead of the private-labeled stuff. As Jeff Bezos has said, "A brand for a company is like a reputation for a person. You earn reputation by trying to do hard things well." Third, I wanted to expand within our territory and acquire more accounts with the help of new salespeople and brokers.

> **You earn reputation by trying to do hard things well**.

The first step was to find good brokers and salespeople to sell our product line. Most of our initial sales were made by only Jan and me. They were small accounts, except for Gourmet Garage. I started to hire salespeople to bring in additional larger customers.

One was a nice man, Ralph. He was fifty years old with white hair, big rings on his hands, and pride in his Italian heritage. He formerly sold cars and was the son of a barber in Bridgeport. After a few years, I had to terminate Ralph due to a lack of acceptable performance. He had a great attitude in sales but had difficulty bringing in significant accounts. When he was let go, he thanked me for keeping him for as long as we did. I found that very strange yet realized he felt overwhelmed in his position and must have known it was only a matter of time before we would need to fill his spot with a more experienced person. We kept in contact for quite a while later.

Paul and Sue were two other salespeople we hired, about a year apart. Paul was from Westchester County, tall and proud of his background in attending culinary school and in working in sales for a distributor in the past. Having been raised in the boroughs of New York, he was street-smart and knew New York City inside and out. He took over the metropolitan accounts and, as Aurora grew, managed one of our biggest accounts at the time, Stop & Shop. Paul was well liked at Aurora. He had a great sense of humor and would roll up his sleeves to help anybody who needed a hand. He stayed with us for over thirteen years and left a couple of years ago. He still calls periodically and has attended our Christmas party since his departure.

Sue started working at Aurora in her late thirties. She was an attractive, blond-haired woman with a wholesome look. She had some previous sales experience working for a commodity company that was one of our vendors and had worked many years for herself, setting up candy stores in malls.

Sue and Paul had the entrepreneurial spirit, both having opened their own shops at one time or another. I liked this spirit because selling to customers utilizes entrepreneurial skills such as independence, thinking on your feet, innovation, and persistence. Neither Sue nor Paul had experience selling to supermarket chains and working with the politics involved, but those things can be learned. The entrepreneurial spirit, on the other hand, needs to come from within. Eventually Paul and Sue became pros and worked together well as a team.

# GROWING CURVE

*Everyone wants to live on top of the mountain, but all the*
*happiness and growth occurs while you're climbing it.*

**—ANDY ROONEY**

Securing a new account is a combination of five factors: need, price, quality, preparation, and timing. All five were at play when I met the buyer for Whole Foods in 2002. It just so happened that they were disappointed in their current supplier of nuts and trail mixes and liked the quality of our product as presented at a trade show. We were in the right place at the right time. They needed a new supplier, our pricing was satisfactory, and we were ready to service them. That was the beginning of a long relationship with Whole Foods.

We started selling to one region and eventually added others. I learned a lot from Whole Foods. Food integrity was critical to them. Every company should have a mission statement or a path that they promote. Quoting from a letter from my pastor after a tour of my facility, "To be a true entrepreneur, a person needs to be a visionary—

to have a clear sense of the kind of person and company you want to be." I got that vision as I continued to follow the parameters outlined by Whole Foods. They represented only all-natural products that did not include artificial ingredients, preservatives, or additives. I agreed with their philosophy of "clean, wholesome food" and was determined that my company's mission would be to offer only the best ingredients that were all-natural or organic. Before meeting Whole Foods, we sold dried fruits with preservatives and candies with artificial colors. We discontinued all those items immediately and followed the philosophy of selling only all-natural and organic food.

> **Every company should have a mission statement or a path that they promote.**

Many people don't understand the difference between organic and all-natural foods. Organic produce is grown in chemical-free soil without pesticides, herbicides, or synthetic fertilizers. It is then processed without the addition of any artificial ingredients or chemicals. All-natural produce can have synthetic fertilizer added to the soil but is processed without artificial additives.

Selling pure, unmodified nuts and dried fruits sets us apart from many of our competitors. Unfortunately Whole Foods was interested only in us packaging our product under their brand, so we were not able to develop our own brand at the time. That was a disappointment since brand identity is critical in building a company, but still we were determined to be the best Whole Foods supplier we could be.

* * *

Around the time we were setting up relationships with buyers at Whole Foods, a food broker, Steve D., approached me with a great opportunity. Steve, I learned, had decided to start his own brokerage company after leaving a large brokerage firm. His first step was to network with manufacturers he had been working with, as well as with decision makers at supermarket chains. His next step was to sell himself to new vendors he wanted to represent.

I wondered how he'd found out about Aurora. As the story goes, one day he was driving on the highway, and he spotted one of our trucks with a picture of our product line on the side panel. This piqued his interest, so as he drove past the vehicle, he wrote down the phone number on the door and called us shortly thereafter. If you knew Steve D., you'd know driving is not his strength. He tends to be a bit absentminded on the road, so I am glad I wasn't in the car with him, or in the vehicle behind him, when he was obtaining that number. He's a determined man, though, which is a testament to his success as a broker.

After getting our number, he called for an appointment. Initially he tried to sell us chocolate from a manufacturer he represented. This wasn't a big business for us, so there was little opportunity at Aurora. However, he eventually came up with a proposal to sell our whole product line to Ahold, the holding company for Stop & Shop, a large supermarket chain in the Northeast. Steve asked for a five-thousand-dollar retainer—a calculated risk for Aurora. I'd been wary of brokers ever since the broker for CRE Designs promised us the moon and delivered a goose egg. Yet I felt Steve was sincere, and he knew people in high managerial positions, including the president of Stop & Shop. So we took the leap, and it was the best thing we ever did for Aurora.

Steve kept his word, and in working with him, he helped me understand how to deal with the big guys at supermarket chains. We worked together in setting up a planogram for displaying over seventy-five items on the shelf in produce. In the early 2000s, most nuts and dried fruits were scattered throughout the store and sold in different packages. Almonds were in pillow bags, apricots in waxy boxes, raisins in regular boxes, granola in pouch bags or cereal boxes, etc. If a consumer wanted to purchase dry-roasted, salted almonds, it would not be easy to identify them based on the packaging.

So with Steve and I working together, Aurora designed a color-coded label system. Green labels or flags suggested salted, orange was for unsalted, and yellow was for raw nuts. Red meant a dried fruit, and blue was for a trail mix. All items were put on the shelf together in uniform, clear PET containers, presenting a plethora of products to choose from. Stop & Shop loved it, and sales soared. The program was so successful that other stores noticed and came on board. Eventually Aurora became the largest customer of Steve's business, and the relationship was mutually beneficial. To this day our companies still work together and have helped each other grow to new heights.

\* \* \*

Soon we were selling our branded items to most supermarket chains in the Northeast as well as private-labeled items to Whole Foods and independent stores. Our brand was getting noticed. Then—wham!— Stop & Shop decided that our brand was selling so well that they wanted to private-label it. Manufacturers don't generally want to private-label as opposed to selling their own brand. First, you lose your market identity. Second, more work is required to keep track of an inventory of different labels and to monitor changeovers when packing on the line. Third, it's easier to lose the customer. You become a packer that can be easily replaced instead of a recognized brand that consumers choose.

Periodically the buyer will send out an RFP (request for proposals), seeking bids from vendors to handle their private-labeled line. I dislike RFPs. They're a lot of work, and they're a bit insulting. You like to think if you are the incumbent and you're doing a great job, the buyer will keep you as the supplier due to loyalty, service, quality, and reasonable pricing.

\* \* \*

Often buyers are unaware of the specs and don't understand that unscrupulous vendors can compromise the agreed-upon standards once they have secured the business and their product is on the shelves. Nuts become a bit smaller than the size bid on, or trail mixes take on more peanuts, in hopes that the buyer or consumer will not notice. Aurora has never done this and has always been consistent with its high specs. It took years for stores to recognize this consistency, and we now have built up a strong reputation for quality, honesty, and character. We tell our customers that there are differences between a juice orange and a navel orange. We explain that if they want quality nuts and specialty items, they should consider Aurora as the purveyor of the navel orange of nuts. Luckily Stop & Shop recognizes our quality and has continued to use Aurora as its provider for private-branded items.

Staying true to our mission has been challenging and may have resulted in some loss of business. Our pricing, although fair, is not the lowest on the shelf. We specialize in top grades of nuts, even in our trail mixes, and these cost more than small or chipped nuts. Our chocolate and vanilla-covered pretzels and nuts contain pure vanilla instead of vanillin, an artificial substitute for vanilla. Our cashews are processed and certified socially compliant, meaning no child labor is used abroad in procuring the nuts. All our nuts are pasteurized, most of them in-house with our own pasteurization system. All this adds to the cost, but the result is worth it. Our quality sets us apart from others. And if a customer decides not to purchase from us because we don't carry the orange-colored apricots with sulfites or the candies with dyes in them, we are disappointed to lose their business but firm in our belief in a high-quality natural product.

\* \* \*

As the years passed, several of our competitors sold out to larger corporations or merged. I've had many opportunities to sell, but Aurora is my baby. I am not in it to count the dollars but rather to enjoy the company's infancy, adolescence, and adulthood. The company was started with little equity. Yet with luck, perseverance, and perhaps help from God, we were able to purchase equipment, trucks, and inventory without long-term loans. Aurora was built on sweat and tears, using cash flow to fund growth.

## Interest is lost money.

If we needed to borrow some money, it was short term and was paid off quickly. Interest is lost money; that's just how I feel. It doesn't mean my way is for everybody. After all if everybody felt that way, there would be no need for venture capital companies or financial institutes.

\* \* \*

Aurora's relationship with our vendors has been vital in securing the best, top-quality products that are reasonably priced. Reputation within the commodity arena is critical, and word spreads fast if you renege on a contract or do not ship out the quality product that was ordered. Jeff, our buyer, has visited many facilities and farms to network with vendors and see how they harvest and process the nuts or fruit. He also looks at their cleanliness and adherence to Safe Quality Food specifications.

Dealing in a pure commodity business is usually based on price rather than on the intrinsic traits of the product. With Aurora, however, we focus on the quality and specifications of the product and represent our line based on value, not only price. Yet price is indeed a significant factor in determining our costs. Some commodities, such as dried fruits, have minimal fluctuation from year to year. Others, such as Brazil nuts, pine nuts, almonds, and walnuts, can fluctuate quite a bit annually.

From 2013 to 2015, California was experiencing a severe drought throughout the state. Not only were lakes drying up but water also was being pumped up from the water table like oil. In 2014, pricing for almonds peaked at over four dollars a pound due to lower yields. Eighty percent of the almonds consumed in the United States come from California. Therefore, with no other source available, manufacturers and distributors were forced to purchase almonds at much higher prices. Today the average wholesale price for almonds is about $2.75.

Brazil nuts also show remarkable variation in price. Brazil nuts are harvested from the Brazil nut tree that grows only in specific Amazon rain forest locations of Bolivia, Brazil, and Peru. Groups of foragers travel into the rainforest to collect the nuts that have dropped from the trees from December until May. Pods containing the nuts are then sorted and processed. A lot of human resources are involved. Today some Brazil nuts are cultivated, but the majority still come from hand foraging. In 2016 a massive drought in the Amazon resulted in a surge in pricing. In other years labor has been short due to political interference, also causing spikes in price. In good years there is plenty of water, and harvesting results in higher yields with lower pricing.

Because we deal with commodities, Aurora needs to adjust pricing regularly to protect itself and make sure the supermarket is getting fair pricing to offer to their consumers. Most of the time, we lock into contracts. This can be good if prices go up, but if prices go down, we are stuck with our commitment.

\* \* \*

Dried fruits tend to fluctuate less in price than nuts, but fruit quality can vary significantly from year to year. We purchase top-grade, organic Turkish figs directly from Turkey. Our vendor and farms have remained the same for years, but the quality differs from crop to crop.

One year we packaged figs for one of our major supermarkets. We received a call a couple of months later saying that they were finding too many body parts within the figs. By body parts they meant the legs and heads of small wasps that pollinate the figs. That year was exceptionally dry in Turkey, and many of the pollinating insects got caught in the fruit. As disgusting as this may sound, the FDA allows up to a certain percentage of these parts in the figs because they are natural to the fruit. We iterated to our customer that the figs were within specifications, but they still didn't like seeing wasp fragments in their fruit. Go figure. We took back the product and resold it to another chain that either didn't notice the parts or understood the fig's growth cycle. We didn't charge them for the extra protein.

\* \* \*

Relationships are critical in working with our vendors. Jeff expects them to supply us with high-quality products and fair pricing.

I'll never forget my first meeting with one of our vendors who sold us cashews and other items. Years ago, around 2000, "Ben" came to visit our company. We were still located in Bridgeport, and the facility was hot and humid from the August weather. He was a young man fully dressed in a black suit and hat in the Hasidic tradition. Our office was not cool enough to avoid getting into a slight sweat if dressed in layers. The air-conditioning worked hard to keep up with the oppressive heat but was half a step behind. Ben had a thick accent from New York's boroughs and brought with him an assortment of salted, unsalted, and raw nuts.

We got along great and were chitchatting away when Cinder, our sheltie at the time, came into the office, yapping at Ben's heels, wanting to play. Ben immediately jumped up on the chair in fear, pleading with us to take the dog away. When we brought Cinder into another office, Ben got off the chair and said, "I can take cats and mice since they are in Brooklyn. Dogs are too scary." He didn't act embarrassed standing on the chair, but I worked hard at keeping a straight face.

After reassuring him that the sheltie was secured in another office, we encouraged him to take off his coat because of the heat. "No, thank you. It is best to keep it on. But I am concerned about this hot weather continuing. I don't like it when my nuts get sweaty." As soon as the words were out of his mouth, he turned beet red with embarrassment—he was, of course, talking about his cashews and almonds. To this day Ben and I are still friends, and Aurora purchases nuts from him periodically. We both chuckle when reminiscing about our first visit.

Over the years Jeff has visited several vendors. One exciting plant he and I visited together was a dried cranberry processor. We started our visit at the bog, where men wade out into the water wearing rubber pants up to their upper chest. They stir the water and the cranberry plants to get the berries to dislodge and rise to the surface for harvesting. We then went into the factory to watch workers sort the debris from the berries.

The cranberries were next put into large freezers, where they were quickly freeze-dried to help rid them of some water and to break down some of their structure. Afterward the freeze-dried cranberries were put into sugar water, where they slowly thawed, absorbing some of the sugared water to sweeten the tartness and give the fruit moisture and texture. If the berries turned out too moist, they were put into a dryer for final processing. It was an interesting process to observe.

Someday I hope to see how dried cherries and blueberries are processed, as dried berries are becoming more popular each year. When I was a child, raisins were the only option available. Now there are dried cherries, cranberries, blueberries, gooseberries, currants, acai, goji, strawberries, elderberries, and more.

Jeff has called on vendors in Vietnam, California, the Himalayas, and several other locations. I personally visited our vendor in Turkey that sells dried figs and apricots, as well as a large almond farm in Spain. Over 80 percent of the almonds eaten in the United States come from California. But Aurora may sometimes purchase almonds from Spain if there is a bad crop in the United States.

\* \* \*

I vividly recall a trip I took with my third husband, Steve, in 2014 to Barcelona. While there, a vendor we were looking into purchasing from invited us to visit his facility and farm. Antonio, the vendor, sent a limousine to pick us up and took about four hours out of his day to show us his processing plant and a couple of his groves and to take us out to lunch. Groves in Spain are much older than those in the United States. The nuts tend to be flatter and a bit larger yet don't have the crunch of American almonds. Bitter almonds, which taste a bit like apricot pits, are often mixed into their product. This is not the case in the United States.

Apricots and almonds belong to the prunus family, known as stone fruits. Members of this family can have a bitter cyanide compound in the seed. For American almonds this bitter taste has been weeded out, whereas in Spain it is acceptable. Often they specifically pick out the bitter almonds from the harvest and use them for marzipan and cookies as opposed to including them as a snack nut.

On our initial introduction, Antonio shook my hand and my husband's. We then went to his office, where I proceeded to talk about our need for almonds and market trends. Every answer he gave to my questions was directed solely at my husband. I received minimal eye contact. After the meeting he took us to a lovely restaurant with Spanish tiles, ceramic floors, and fish tanks from which you could pick your meal if you chose. During the whole lunch, Antonio barely addressed me. He was wooing my husband, making sure he was comfortable, calling over the waiter to introduce him, having him choose the fish, and describing to him the correct way to eat Spanish oysters. Sitting outside and reading a book would have been more rewarding to me than sitting there, being ignored. When we left, Antonio's chauffeur drove us back to Barcelona.

Although appreciative of the time and attention Antonio had given us, I was quite frustrated. I felt dismissed, both as a woman and as a potential customer. I was not sure whether his issue was cultural or personal. When we got back to the hotel, I emailed a thank-you note to Antonio, adding, "Next time you come to the United States, please bring your wife to Aurora. We would love to meet her and give both of you a tour of our facility. We can then perhaps invite you to our home."

His response to me was short and concise: "Thank you. Also, make sure you bring your husband. Although he does not own Aurora, you need him to give you good advice." That was the end of our relationship, and we never purchased from him again.

# TRADE SHOWS

*A trade show is a great
focus group for your product.*

– SUE MONHAIT

Trade shows are a great way to lure prospective customers into your booth and introduce them to your product line. Trade shows, conventions, and expositions focus on a particular industry and feature keynote speakers, events, vendor displays, and other activities of interest to attendees in a common segment. For Aurora there are a couple of industry segments that hold our interest. One is gourmet foods; the other is produce.

The perfect trade show for gourmet foods and innovative concepts is the Fancy Food Show, held twice a year. We always either host a booth of our own at the show—held at the Javits Center in New York City—or, at a minimum, attend the show and visit all the booths. You never know what new ideas you'll find when looking at the various stalls.

At the Fancy Food Show, all sorts of artisan exhibitors try to capture as many buyers as possible for their products. Items include gourmet chocolates, cookies, smoked fish, olives, flowers, labels, cheeses, pâtés, as well as a myriad of other specialty items. If a buyer comes to your booth from a leading supermarket chain, you use every marketing skill you possess to motivate them to purchase your item. All you need is one fruitful lead, and the show is well worth the money spent.

For Aurora the Fancy Food Show is fun and not too expensive when we choose to exhibit. In total the price is usually less than five thousand dollars, which includes the exhibit and all additional accessories, such as carpet, lighting, table and chairs, and wastebasket. Several seminars are offered for participants, although I'm not usually one to attend these since I can barely get through them without nodding off. The show is an excellent place for networking, however.

One advantage of the Fancy Food Show is that it's only seventy-five miles from our location. So none of our people need to stay at hotels or rent cars, and everyone gets to sleep in their own beds during the three- or four-day show. I believe the Fancy Food Show is where Aurora first met the buyer from Whole Foods, which has been one of our best accounts for the past fifteen years. I have nothing but great things to say about the Fancy Food Show and the wonderful leads it has provided us.

* * *

The second segment we pursue at trade shows is the produce segment. Most of Aurora's product line is presented in the produce section of supermarkets or in the grocery section that borders produce. The largest show we attend for produce is the Produce Marketing Association (PMA) Fresh Summit, held annually. This show moves around from year to year. This year it is in New Orleans, which is a lot of fun. We all love going to the French Quarter when the show ends for the day. Past locations have included Anaheim, Atlanta, and Houston.

The first few times you attend the PMA, you are in awe of all the glitzy displays. You see people with Mexican hats representing a salsa company, a woman in a banana costume walking around as Miss Chiquita, and young people giving out samples of juice, guacamole, grapes, salads, and trail mixes, as well as a festival of nifty hats, massage chairs, and costumes. The smells are enticing as you pass a booth making hot dogs with their special sauce or fresh pizza with basil. People line up to get free samples, chatting away and networking with one another. The sushi exhibit, where they display soy sauce, has always been my favorite. Often I'll go to the booth to get a sample and then send one of my salespeople to get me a second one to avoid being seen in line again. I usually skip breakfast and lunch when attending this show. There's so much grazing at the various booths that I'm sure my calorie demand is met by the end of the day.

At the PMA show, there are many seminars for those who choose to attend. There are also fun games and events at various booths that attract crowds. At the end of the day, our team goes out for a nice meal with cocktails and unwinds while sharing stories of the people they met at the show and the leads they need to follow. Trade shows can be dangerous if you relax too much in the evening. After the effort of keeping a smile on your face all day, it is easy to enjoy a martini or two. After the third, watch out. You don't want to act foolishly in front of your customers who may be seated at your table.

Aurora has had a booth at the PMA Fresh Summit almost every year for the past fifteen years. We spend a lot of money on the space for our booth and accessories, as well as transportation and housing for three of us to staff the booth. Also, the display panels we bring from home and the whole pallet of our goodies that we set up in the booth are pretty costly. At the end of the show, we donate our nuts and snacks to the food bank rather than pay to ship them back home.

The show can be a lot of fun but also very tiring when you stand on your feet for eight hours, two or three days in a row.

Initially the trade show was great for soliciting new business. Paul was especially skilled at bringing people into our booth. He was our "hook man." When someone walked by with a badge reading "Buyer from XYZ Supermarket Chain," they didn't stand a chance. He would stick out his invisible hook and escort them into our booth to discuss our nuts and how their chain needed our product. After a few years, the trade show became a way for us to network and set up meetings with buyers for existing customers, especially if we hadn't seen them for a while. It's a great time to socialize and cement relationships.

> **The shows are fun but not always fruitful for successful small businesses. For larger corporations they are a must.**

We still do trade shows, but now we periodically skip a year or two to get some rest. The shows are fun but not always fruitful for successful small businesses. For larger corporations they are a must to set up meetings with their customers and to maintain their presence.

# SOCIAL AND NETWORKING EVENTS

*If you want to go somewhere, it is best to meet*
*someone who has already been there.*

**—ROBERT KIYOSAKI**

O ver the past twenty years, I have been asked to be a guest speaker or adjunct speaker for many events. Most of them are women's networking events, entrepreneurial workshops, chambers of commerce, or universities. I enjoy giving speeches and expressing the importance of passion in entrepreneurial endeavors. I tell the audience that the most challenging part of bringing a business to great heights is finding something that grabs you. That is your primary driver. As Oprah Winfrey has said, "Let passion drive your profession." Without it you just have a job.

I have met many people at these events, particularly women who want to set up their businesses but don't know how. I try to help in ways that I can but am most helpful for people who are interested in manufacturing and selling a commodity or food product. The only unpleasant aspects of these functions are the calls and solicitations after the event from insurance brokers, bankers, and other professionals trying to sell me their services. Ivan Misner once said, "Networking is more about farming than it is about hunting." That may be so, but I feel hunted when I get solicitations after being a guest speaker.

> The most challenging part of bringing a business to great heights is finding something that grabs you.

In 2012 I was honored as a member of the Hall of Fame for Junior Achievement of Western Connecticut. The mission of Junior Achievement is to inspire and prepare young students to succeed in their endeavors. When notified that I would be given such an outstanding award, I wasn't sure why I deserved it. Award winners are usually local people who serve as an inspiration and example to students.

The board explained to me that a woman-owned business around the city of Bridgeport was important because it illustrated to the youth that it could be done. Bridgeport is a poor city that at one time declared bankruptcy. It is home to many misguided and insecure youths who are often raised by one parent or grandparent. If a local woman could set up her own business, why couldn't they? It made sense for me to be honored. I still have the bronze award sitting on my fireplace mantel in my home office, and I'm proud of it.

Since receiving the award, Aurora continues to invite youths to our facility each year for a tour. Afterward we have a contest to see who can make the most exciting trail mix from ingredients put on the table. Last but not least, we have a short question and answer session to reinforce what they have learned. It's a lot of fun. Many people at Aurora participate. At the end of the session, we take a group picture of the children and staff to put on our wall. I sometimes wonder if we've made an impact on any of the children who have come through the facility. If just one child were inspired, it would be worth all the time we put into this function each year.

* * *

A couple of years after starting Aurora, I began to feel that being certified as a woman-owned business would be beneficial. Being certified as woman owned requires a female to own and control at least 51 percent of the business. The application is lengthy and requires forms ranging from tax returns to a list of assets. After you submit all forms, the certifying organization sends a representative to meet you and make sure everything is valid. If your business is a widget manufacturer, the representative may ask you what your most expensive widget sells for and who will purchase it. You had better know the answer. Husband and wife teams can be deceiving, as many husbands want to put the business in their wife's name to use it as an advantage.

For Aurora being certified as woman owned has been advantageous only as a plus for supermarkets that strive to maintain quotas of minority-owned businesses. Periodically I'll get a call from one of our larger chains asking if they can do a small write-up on me with a picture to emphasize to their customers that they are diversity motivated. To my recollection I have never been awarded a business contract because of my certification. Maybe someday, though, a customer seeking a woman-owned snack company will invite Aurora into their stores. And—who knows?—perhaps some of the companies currently purchasing our products continue to do so because we're considered a minority-owned business.

* * *

When looking back to my early years at Aurora Products, it seems that I worked over seventy hours a week. Weekends and weekdays merged together as one, except the weekend was a bit quieter. Eventually I realized I could use somebody to bounce ideas off to assure that management, which was primarily me, was heading in the right direction. Since we did not have a board of advisors, I decided to join a Vistage group.

> **Sometimes it gets lonely at the top, and you need someone to listen to you and give you advice.**

Vistage is a peer-mentoring group whose members discuss business and personal issues. It comprises CEOs, business owners, and decision-making executives of small to midsize companies. It is not inexpensive to become a member, but the cost is worth the benefit for some executives. Sometimes it gets lonely at the top, and you need someone to listen to you and give you advice.

Although the meetings were informative, especially the part where we would go around the room to discuss issues in our company with our ten to twelve group members, the guest speakers were not of much interest to me. Most of the time, they were motivational speakers discussing topics ranging from social media promotions to employee incentives to weight loss. With my attention deficit, I just could not pay attention without nodding off. The meetings were monthly and would fill up a whole day. That's a lot of time for me to invest.

Many members of my group were enjoyable to talk to. Yet I felt disappointed that they did not understand my business as a manufacturer/distributor or wholesaler. Most members were from accounting firms, hospitals, printing companies, social media firms, advertising agencies, insurance companies, employment agencies, and other service businesses, although periodically there would be a manufacturer. They tried to be helpful, and I met my new accountant at one of my groups. He was a member and knew quite a bit about Aurora by the time we engaged him, which occurred only after I left the group.

I belonged to two separate Vistage groups over the years. I left the first group after becoming disheartened that the coach had no understanding of how my business grew. She was a woman who did her consulting work by the book, if indeed there was such a book. In discussing my business, she said, "It's amazing how well Aurora has done. It is serendipitous how successful you have become. You would certainly be a unique case for Harvard to look at."

What did she mean by that? I took it as she thought I was lucky that Aurora had succeeded despite not following all the rules, such as having a large board, a CFO, projections, and audited returns. I told her the success of Aurora was based on hard work, perseverance, following advice, getting good people, and having the essential ingredient—passion. It was not pure luck. The only serendipitous part was finding the opportunity—which was what motivated me to name this book *Serendipity or Passion?* What I *did* with the luck of finding a great opportunity was up to me. I eventually left her group, not primarily because of the remark but to get into a group closer to home. After three years with the second group, I left due to the time commitment, but I still stay in touch with some of the people.

# MY ENCOUNTER
# WITH IMUS

*I talk to millions of people every day;*
*I just like it when they can't talk back.*

‒DON IMUS

I n 2007 I got a phone call from a marketing woman representing WFAN Radio. She was looking to see if we were interested in advertising on the *Imus in the Morning* radio show. We were thinking we should be more aggressive in our advertising, so the proposition sounded interesting. I was not a huge fan of WFAN since it was a sports channel and I can barely tell the difference between soccer and cricket, but I enjoyed listening to the banter and the exciting guests on Imus's show. He was a legend, and I thought it would be great for him to mention Aurora in his program. I thought the advertising

## Advertising might open up awareness of our brand.

might open up awareness of our brand. So I told them I was interested, and they set up an appointment for me to meet Imus.

My son Matthew and I drove into New York City and were escorted into Imus's office. We brought a huge box of samples for Imus and his staff to enjoy. The office was dimly lit with a couch on one end and a plush sitting chair opposite Imus's desk. After we sat down, Imus came strutting in with his cowboy boots, hat, and western attire. I always pictured him as a large man, but he was shorter and slighter than I envisioned. He was also quite wrinkled, probably from the sun on his Arizona ranch.

I was nervous and just started chatting about how excited I was to meet him. I told him my husband George was sorry he couldn't make it into the city to meet him since he was a great fan of Imus. His response? "Is George your son's father?"

"No," I answered. "Matthew's father is named Dick. George is his stepfather."

I proceeded to talk about the growth of Aurora and how it emerged from Amalgamated and about growing sprouts with Dick. I said how George had been helpful to me when starting Aurora and how Matthew was now part of Aurora's team. When I finished talking about Amalgamated and Aurora, as well as Dick, George, and Matthew, I think Imus was a bit amused and perhaps confused.

After a while he called his salespeople into the office. When they entered, he remarked, "These salespeople are slower than molasses and should be shot."

Then he took a gun from the drawer of his desk and tentatively laid it on the desk. "Nah, I'll do it later." I'm guessing this was all an act since I never heard any news about salespeople being gunned down, but it was amusing. I will never forget what an entertaining man he was.

One week later my ads started on the radio, where Imus would talk about Aurora and how delicious and wholesome our nuts and snacks were. I was so delighted to hear our name come from the lips of Imus, that is, until he blurted out, "Yeah. I met the owner of the company, a nice lady, but she doesn't know who her husband is. She kept talking about her husband Dick and her husband George."

I was embarrassed. I called immediately and told them to please speak to Imus and ask him not to say things like that. I did not want to be embarrassed again nor have people think I was ditzy. The marketing woman told me that, luckily, Imus liked us, and we were fortunate he didn't say anything worse. She also told me she would talk to him and ask him to be careful in what he said.

Thankfully George never heard this one ad, or if he did, he didn't say anything. Imus was spontaneous and said whatever he wanted to without thinking of the consequences. That was what made him so interesting to listen to, that is, until he made an offhanded comment about the African American players on Rutgers women's basketball team, which came across as racist. He was fired. The sales team asked me if I wanted to continue with the advertising, but it wasn't the same without Imus. They refunded my money.

# FAMILY MEMBERS
# AT AURORA

*You have to respect your parents. They are giving
you an at bat. If you're an entrepreneur and go into
the family business, you want to grow fast. Patience
is important. But respect the other party.*

**—GARY VAYNERCHUK**

At work everybody knew about my family. Nothing was private. When my kids were upset about something—a problem at school or something annoying a sibling did— they would not think twice about coming into my office to discuss it instead of waiting until I came home. As they got older, most problems subsided, but still the office held no secrets.

Owning a family business with children who work for you can be challenging. As my children grew up, they all worked for Aurora at one time or another. They started as teens making a little extra money for gas or college. Most of the time, they would make labels in the office or help file, at least for starters. But they might end up being relegated to the production floor with white hairnets, vinyl gloves, and plastic aprons, particularly if I noticed they were fraternizing too much or distracting others in the office with their teenage chatter. I enjoyed taking the kids to work with me. At least I knew where they were, and they were learning work ethics.

As a young teenager, my son would come to work with me. Being a bit immature, he would sneak any free time when Mom was not looking to play with the computer. Many times we had to call the IT specialist, and we'd be told the computer system was down because games containing a virus were loaded on the system, or some other teen-traceable problem had occurred.

One time my traffic manager came to my office a bit embarrassed. Somebody had put a screen saver on his computer of a naked man about an inch tall chasing a half-naked woman across the screen. Who do you suppose had done it? My beloved son, of course. He thought it was funny.

Today he is a mature man and does not like to be reminded of his earlier pranks and indiscretions. Yet here it is, written in this book for everybody to read. Mothers can be so cruel.

In 2017 Gregory got his bachelor's degree and started working for Aurora as manager of safety and compliance. He had a lot to learn since coursework at his school did not include safety compliance. After additional studies, he earned his certification as a safety professional while working at Aurora. Greg is now an expert in his field and pursuing his master's degree.

Gregory's position is an excellent fit for him and our company. He takes care of safety issues as well as insurance—dealing with workers' compensation and liabilities—and has brought Aurora's safety protocols to a new level. As a result of his efforts, our workers' compensation rates have declined.

The safety department ensures Aurora follows protocol with hazardous chemicals used in cleaning equipment. It also enforces compliance with "lock out/tag out" procedures to prevent anybody from working on a defective piece of equipment while it is being repaired. Greg is an asset to Aurora and is invaluable in maintaining OSHA compliance. This is not easy due to the many rules and regulations requiring constant attention. Aurora feels safe under his watchful eyes.

In the summer of 2005, Matthew started working for Aurora. Although it was an injustice to him in retrospect, Matthew was a godsend to me. It is usually better for children to work away from home for a least five years before joining a family-run business. Nobody at Aurora could teach him about operations, engineering, industrial knowledge, or management since we were all new in our jobs. He had to learn independently, but he was a quick study. He helped organize Aurora and took a big load off my shoulders. The many responsibilities of running the company were overwhelming and affecting my health.

Matthew arranged production meetings, worked with trucking, and took a leadership role. He was eventually promoted to vice president of operations and was a great help in this role and in our moves to Stratford and Orange. I don't know what I would have done without Matthew at the time. Probably keel over from anxiety and overwork. He became such an integral part of Aurora.

My daughter Laura came to work for me in 2010 after receiving her MBA from Fordham. Like her father her interests lay in marketing, yet she was also excellent in sales. Having worked for a food broker in sales before graduate school, she did not lack confidence. Laura is a smart woman and was offered the vice presidency of a division of a food brokerage firm at twenty-six. It was an honor for her, being so young. It was difficult for Laura and me to work together and to differentiate Mom from the boss. Also, she and Matthew were competitive and were both looking for their foothold.

When kids graduate from school with an MBA, they sometimes feel they have the education to teach or lead others. Yes, Laura had the degree, but she had a way to go before understanding Aurora's marketing and sales needs. Aurora needed a good salesperson, not a marketer. However, Laura was determined to spend her time marketing our product.

Eventually she got tired of working with her family and decided to move on. She took a managerial position with Chobani in sales and left Aurora. Both she and I were pleased with this decision. I loved her, but we needed separation, and I believed she needed to follow her own path and to gain more experience away from family.

Eight or nine years later, Laura returned to Aurora and is now a great asset. Her marketing and sales skills are top notch, and she takes care of our most challenging and prominent customers. Timing—in addition to talent and ability to work together as a team—is critical when it comes to family working with family. Laura augments me with her abilities and surpasses my sales skills.

> **Timing—in addition to talent and ability to work together as a team—is critical when it comes to family working with family.**

Lindsay, my fourth child, worked for Aurora Products periodically as a teenager and young adult to earn extra money. As a grown woman, she worked at Aurora as a retail representative. After a year of working for us, she decided to move on to other things and spread her wings.

\* \* \*

I would be remiss in telling this story without mentioning the four-legged family members that have worked, or are still working, at Aurora, keeping everybody company. My family has always had two Shetland sheepdogs at a time. These dogs have brought me happiness and calm over the years.

Aurie was named after Aurora Products. I loved his personality, intelligence, and size, so we decided to breed him with Bella, our sweet female sheltie. Everybody waited eagerly for the day the pups would be born. Finally Bella gave birth to four tiny puppies. All the employees got to enjoy the puppies as they developed. Every morning I would bring Bella into work with the puppies in a plastic container designed to hold six to eight large potatoes at a supermarket or, as they got bigger, in a carrier. Then they would all be put into a pen in my office where Bella could nurse her pups and employees could come by and admire her brood.

One of the criteria for new hires working in the office at Aurora is that they like dogs. Dogs are our mascots and earn their keep by making everybody happy with their wagging tails. If a person doesn't like dogs, they won't mesh into our casual culture and will be annoyed by the occasional barking when visitors come to the door or by a furry nose arriving on their lap for a treat.

Although the dogs bring me delight, they can do embarrassing things, such as barking loudly when I'm on a conference call or playfully trying to herd employees walking into work. Then there was the time, around 2011, when we had an important meeting at our facility with a buyer and her associates from Whole Foods. We were all nervous and anxious to have a successful meeting. Everyone was dressed appropriately, the office was cleaned, and a welcome sign was mounted at the front desk for our important visitors. When the buyer first came into the building, she greeted Aurie. She thought he was so cute and playfully pet him.

An hour later, as we were all sitting around the conference table, discussing important business issues, she kept shifting uncomfortably in her chair, moving her legs around. I thought she was just a bit restless until she finally blurted out, "Is there a way you can please have your dog stop humping my leg?" Sure enough, under the table, Aurie was showing her leg some personal attention. This did not help with our presentation, and we were very embarrassed. Aurie was not happy that we put him in my office to keep him away from his favorite hobby.

Over the years we've had some employees who bring their dogs to work. In addition, we have Ollie, the fish that lives in our controller's office, and Jeff's water frogs, which he keeps in a bowl in his office. At Aurora animals are family.

* * *

Unfortunately, not all family members are permanent. When George and I were married in 1995, he was a good friend. We helped each other in business, as well as raised six children together. After the children left the family nest, we drifted apart. In October 2011 George looked at me and said, "You don't want to be married to me anymore, do you?" I love him for that. We got divorced in early 2013. I loved the new freedom I felt. I had a business I loved, children I adored, and the freedom to go out if I wanted.

After dating several men through the internet, I met my third and final husband through Match.com. I never planned on getting married again; my intention was only to have fun and perhaps find someone to go out with. But Steve won my heart. He was totally different from my other husbands. Both my ex-hubbies were businessmen and very competitive. Steve was a Renaissance man who enjoyed life to the fullest. He had no interest in business and had no sense for money matters. He lacked the social comparison gene of worrying about what the neighbors were doing and wanting to have more than they had. In his youth he'd been an actor on Broadway and owned an outdoor canoe shop. He was also, at various times, an accountant, teacher, carpenter, plumber, and car salesman. If I were to delve further into his life, it would take another chapter, so let's just say that I could not resist Steve. He augments me. They always say the third time is the charm, and for me they were right. We got married on July 4, 2014.

# THEFT

*The worst feeling in the world is to feel betrayed by
someone you thought was a friend and had your back.*

— M E

In 2007 business was hectic. Matthew helped a lot in operations, but I was still short-staffed in dealing with the company's growth. My blood pressure was out of control. A thirty-something woman whom I will call Sherry came to work for Aurora. She was a quick study and had a charismatic smile. She would sometimes tell me how, when she was younger, her mother would get angry at her antics, including club-hopping, car accidents without insurance, and general lack of responsibility. She claimed to have grown up a lot since then.

I liked Sherry and took her under my wing and into my family. She was my assistant, and she also served as human resource manager. I desperately needed her to help me with the loads of work I had on my plate. I thought she had my back and was protecting my interests.

As time went on, there were signs that things were not going right with Sherry. Some temporary employees who had come and gone from Aurora reported getting W-2s for wages they never earned. Items were being purchased at Staples that I did not remember authorizing. I would bring it up to Sherry, but she would somehow wiggle out of the situation with some explanation or other that seemed to make sense.

One day she told me she was taking a week off for vacation. While she was gone, I checked her email, as was commonly done when looking for work-related issues, and opened a verification notice for mileage taken out of my AmEx card for first-class tickets to New Orleans. Sherry had access to my account and had used my points without asking. What else was she doing?

When I approached her, she seemed almost relieved. Her life was out of control, she told me, and she recognized she needed help. She was stealing from Aurora in multiple ways. She was claiming false hours for employees from the temp agency and cashing the checks herself. She was also using my credit card for expenses and for purchasing cameras, coats, rental cars, and even manicures for herself and her friends. I wondered why she was so attentive in taking my dogs to the vet. It was because she had cats that needed to be seen too, and she led the vet to believe they were mine.

Her theft amounted to over $220,000. I was not angry, just sad and embarrassed. I felt like such a fool for not spotting this earlier. How could I be so vulnerable and stupid? Regardless, I reported Sherry's theft, and she went to jail for a couple of years. She admitted she had a drug problem and needed to work through it.

Today she periodically visits me, and has two children in addition to the son she had while working for me. She appears to be happy. She tells me that the lesson she learned was invaluable. I hope so.

\* \* \*

I still wonder how this theft got past me. It took place over three years. Why didn't I spot it? In retrospect, when a business owner is so overwhelmed and desperate, they are often so relieved to have someone step in and help alleviate the stress that they are blinded. Sherry was that person for me. I had blind faith during a hectic time. I was working over seventy hours a week and couldn't see the forest for the trees.

In addition to having money and services stolen, we've had a load of nuts hijacked. In 2015 we ordered a truckload of almonds from California. This load was worth over a hundred thousand dollars. It just vaporized. The trucking company we hired arranged for a pickup, signed off on the goods, and then disappeared. In my younger years, television sets and computers would be stolen by large professional theft rings. Now it is nuts.

Today we have steps to help deter and prevent theft. Our ERP and accounting systems have checks and balances that were not in place years ago. These systems integrate inventory with purchase orders and tie different departments and functions together, allowing cross-checking to occur. We also have checks and balances in human resources that would not allow what Sherry did in the past to happen without being noticed.

> **We have steps to help deter and prevent theft.**

The most frustrating type of theft that occurs for us is the legal kind—having our ideas and product concepts stolen. You work hard to develop new items through research and development, only to turn around and see the same product in the store with a competitor's label on it. It's been said that the best compliment to pay someone is to imitate them. This may be true, but it makes it hard to compete when others lift your ideas. We introduced our Salad Fixins as a new product, and it sold like wildfire. The next thing I knew, everybody was offering salad toppers. They couldn't use our trade name since we had it registered, but they sure used our concept.

# PEOPLE DYNAMICS

*Coming together is a beginning, staying together is progress, and working together is success.*

**—HENRY FORD**

One of the things I enjoy the most at Aurora is the camaraderie in the office and on the production floor. With over 180 employees working in the production area, there are bound to be arguments and issues, but most employees work hard together to support their families.

When you work together, everybody knows what is going on with everyone else. Friendships and relationships are formed, but fights also break out when someone feels disrespected or thinks someone is after their man. Things can get touchy, especially in the summer when the weather is hot. Yet I still love going on the production line to see employees working hard (well, most of them). Although I no longer know all their names, I recognize most of them and greet them with a smile. Aurora needs every person who works there. Without good employees we are nothing.

Often we have company meetings in the lunchroom with all employees. In starting the session, I usually introduce myself to all newcomers and remind them that we all need to work together—after all many of us see one another more than we do our own families. Although most people have seen me at Aurora, newcomers may wonder what this white-haired woman is doing wandering around. Is she somebody's mother? Is she lost?

> **Without good employees we are nothing.**

With so many employees working together, it is occasionally difficult to keep things copacetic. Sometimes I feel sorry for Janice or Colleen, who comprise our human resource department. Much of their work seems to be addressing people's gripes with appropriate actions that Aurora should take. Last week, for example, an employee claimed that another employee's family followed her home with threats. We have no lack of drama in the warehouse, and human resources often takes the role of mediator more than it should.

*  *  *

Sometimes racism is brought up, and Aurora tries to mediate. We require a two-hour training on harassment and discrimination, but it's hard to manage everybody's feelings and versions of the truth. We had a lawsuit from an employee alleging we let her go because she was Hispanic. The suit had nothing to go on since 35 percent of our employees are Hispanic. She lost the case, but when things go to court, everybody loses. Sensitivity to race and color is an ongoing issue, with so many employees working together in a confined space on a day-to-day basis.

Several employees at Aurora come from different countries such as Costa Rica, Dominican Republic, Ghana, Mexico, Haiti, and other areas. Most of the employees in production don't earn a lot, yet some still manage to save some money to send to their families abroad. I'm not used to that—many people here in Connecticut feel that Mom and Dad should support *them*, not the other way around.

One employee came into my office asking to borrow five thousand dollars from his 401(k) plan. The official withdrawal criteria were not met because the money was to be used to help his brother's wife in Ghana while her husband was in the hospital, recuperating from an illness. I liked this man; he had worked at Aurora for several years and was highly respected. So I gave him the money. When he realized it was a gift, he dropped to his knees on my office floor, teary-eyed. I was taken aback. I thought of the money simply as a bonus for a good man who needed funds for his family, the right thing to do. To him it was everything. It was survival for his family. This is one reason I love working with the people at Aurora. We may have drama, but there is a lot of compassion as well.

Among the office staff, I know of Diana's love for collecting knick-knacks (which I tease her by calling it "hoarding"), Candy's frustrations with her older daughter who is entering the terrible adolescent years, Jeff and Rick's love of fishing, Chris's new purchase of a home, and how Jason—who is Italian and married to an Asian woman—loves to sneak Italian food and drink coffee instead of his wife's native cuisine. Everybody in the office knows who hogs the bathroom for their midmorning read, who likes to sneak onto Facebook every morning, and who loves to bake. They all know about my family, how I love martinis, and how I look forward to going home to my husband, who cooks great food.

\* \* \*

Over the years we have had many parties at the company. In the early days, we took all employees and their families to Lake Compounce, a recreational park, for fun and laughter. After a while the company got too big, and we had smaller parties.

I especially enjoyed the Christmas meals where all employees in the production area would bring a special dish to share. I loved the seasonings Elba would put in her pork and the tasty rice dishes brought in by other women. I loved Elba's pork so much that every Easter she would give me a gift of large, seasoned pork, and all I had to do was throw it in my oven at home for my large family on the Sunday holiday. I got so many compliments that I decided not to tell them it was a gift from Elba. If you were familiar with my cooking, you'd understand why I needed all the compliments I could get.

\* \* \*

In addition to having over two hundred full-time employees for the past ten years, Aurora also employs several temporary employees on a temp-to-hire basis. We do this so as to vet employees, ensuring they can follow instructions and adhere to all our safe food handling protocols. Also, many temporary employees tend to jump from job to job, and we don't want to invest in training them unless they stay. Often we can have up to a hundred temps working.

Aurora helps the Kennedy Center by paying its clients piecemeal for hand-filling our tubs. The Kennedy Center is an organization that helps mentally challenged people who need jobs and can work with guidance. Their ages range from twenty-one to sixty-five. Although they work at one-fifth the production rate of our hired employees, they do a good job and are thrilled to be helpful.

They come to work with smiles and lunch boxes in a van driven by their supervisor or coach. During the day the coach makes sure they stay seated at their worktables. If they need to use the restroom, the coach will accompany them. Over the years we have had a few glitches, but the clients of the Kennedy Center are a delight to work with, and everybody in the facility is pleased to see them. We try to incorporate them into our regular workforce as much as possible.

# NEW PRODUCT
# DEVELOPMENT

*Don't find customers for your products;*
*find products for your customers.*

− SETH GODIN

To continue growing and expanding in stores, Aurora needs to routinely offer new products. Sales are important, but we always need new items to keep the buyers' interest. Buyers want to know you're on the cutting edge of development. For the first ten years, I essentially comprised the research and development department. This was the part of my job that I loved the most. My focus group to test new items consisted of office staff and factory employees. Maybe the years spent as a scientist and researcher prepped me in some way?

Sometime around 2004 I put together a mix that I thought would be great on a salad. I noticed that most salad bars offered sunflower seeds, sesame sticks, raisins, dried cranberries, and almond slices for people to sprinkle on their salads. I thought, *Why not offer this same mix to the consumer?* I put the blend together and gave it to one of our brokers representing New Jersey supermarkets. He assured me he would present the product to ShopRite or one of the other chains.

Six months later while visiting him at his office, I noticed the container still sitting on his desk. I was annoyed and realized that this broker was not the best person to represent our product line. Having a new item accepted at a store requires cooperation and enthusiasm in your salespeople as well as in the buyer. The product could be a great one, but if it is not shown or does not grab the buyer's interest, you have to consider the item dead or on hold for another time. In this particular case, I put the item on hold and kept a container on my shelf.

About six months later, Steve D., the broker who represented me at Stop & Shop and was very enthusiastic about our product line, asked me if I had any new ideas to show his accounts. I always tell my sales staff, "Never go empty handed when visiting a buyer." I quickly grabbed the container from my shelf and handed it to him.

"Nice," he said. "What a great idea!"

He presented the item to the buyer, and they loved it. We named the product Salad Fixins and cross-marketed it with lettuce and other salad items. It was a hit.

\* \* \*

Eventually I introduced a larger package size to BJ's Wholesale Club, and they sold the Salad Fixins for a few years under our brand until swapping it to their own private label. It was a creative item at the time. Now salad toppers are being sold in a lot of stores.

We got other products into warehouse clubs, but these were basically "in and out" programs where they would introduce the item for a short period, perhaps three months, and then discontinue it. If the product sold well, they might bring it back at another time; or if the item flew off the shelf, they might want to keep it as a permanent offering. Being in a warehouse club gives you visibility and a chance for significant sales.

Dealing with warehouse clubs is risky though. If the product succeeds, you can make a lot of money. But if it is discontinued, you may be left with a large inventory of bags and boxes made specifically for that particular club. This has happened to us more than once. One time, for example, BJ's Wholesale Club told us they had another supplier for our Salad Fixins. At this time we were private-labeling for them. When they stopped ordering, we were left with over ten thousand dollars' worth of bags and corrugated trays with BJ's name on them. Our dumpster was full that week.

Wholesale clubs can also unintentionally sabotage your products. An item we showed to Sam's Wholesale Club was our Grail Mix, a combination of granola and trail mix. They told us it would be sold in the New England area, which we thought was great. There are many healthy food lovers who eat granola up here. We were excited and knew the product would sell well in Maine or Massachusetts, particularly in the winter months, as was promised.

Well, after many delays and much procrastination on their part, Sam's decided to sell the product through their warehouses in Texas and neighboring Southern states in August instead. Who eats granola in Texas in the heat of the summer? It's like selling ice cream in Alaska during a cold front. You can imagine what happened. Grail Mix was a flop and a great disappointment. Sam's tried to have us take back the unsellable surplus, but we refused due to the location and timing of their release to the market.

\* \* \*

In 2011 we decided to set up an official research and development division that could develop new ideas and concepts and continually fine-tune the processes we had in place. For this position we hired Roshna. Roshna was responsible for coming up with new ideas, creating formulas for trail mixes, and helping Aurora become more vertically integrated.

Up till this time, we'd been purchasing granola from a company in Michigan, which did our baking. However, the freight costs, supply, consistency of the product, distance, and timeliness of deliveries became issues. Consequently we began to source out local bakeries to see if we could purchase a company closer to Aurora to make our bestselling granola, Vanilla Crunch, as well as our other varieties. After a few months of searching to no avail, we gave up.

*Why not make our own?* we thought. If we made granola in-house, we would gain independence while saving money. We would also gain control over the quality and consistency of the product. Roshna was assigned the task. Our new bakery would need to be able to keep up with our sales volume and earn approval by the health department. We purchased three large ovens, a mixer, trays, and all the other necessary equipment, and we did the building alterations.

With the help of an outside firm, Roshna spent weeks in the kitchen helping develop our granola, and now—trying to speak objectively, of course—we have the best granola in all the stores. After a hard day, I love leaving the factory and smelling the aroma of freshly baked granola as it is coming out of the ovens.

* * *

The research and development department also spent months developing the protocol and recipe for Bavarian roasted nuts. Roasting butter-toasted peanuts and glazed honey nuts entails a precise process. Our two Bavarian roasters are large copper kettles that heat a mixture of honey, butter, sugar, and water to a specific temperature. When it is just right, you add the nuts you want to glaze. The blending paddles constantly go around in the large kettle, distributing the slurry and preventing the nuts from burning. If the heat is on for too long, the nuts burn. If the timing is too short, the nuts don't get glazed enough, and they aren't crispy. When the nuts are ready, they are spread out on a cooling table and allowed to cool down for about fifteen minutes before being put into a blue bin to be taken into the cooler and packed within the next few days. The aroma from Bavarian roasted nuts is mouthwatering.

Sometimes a product development cycle at Aurora results in an item that fails. For example, we created smoothie mixes that contained nuts, grains, and dried fruits in attractive bags. It took us a year to develop the product and packaging and to do the required tastings, but only one store purchased the line.

Another failure was one of my favorites, the "roast your own nuts" package. In a pouch bag of sliced almonds, we placed a small packet of Tuscan-flavored olive oil. The consumer was directed to add the oil to the nuts in a frying pan and sauté them for five minutes. They tasted so good. I don't think people understood this product, and Aurora did not have the marketing funds to advertise or educate the consumer. Sadly it was carried in only one chain and then dropped due to lack of sales.

One of the least complicated items to bring to market is a new trail mix blend that follows a trend. For example, our Paleo Mix was a hit when the Paleo diet was a fad. A Paleo diet typically includes lean meat, fish, fruits, vegetable seeds, and nuts. It contains those foods found during the caveman era before farming. Now the trend is keto and dark chocolate. A ketogenic diet consists of high fat, low carbohydrates. By eating a high-fat diet, the body is forced to metabolize fat rather than carbohydrates. Mixes that contain coconut or our Bavarian roasted nuts are also the trend.

Our latest development is our Grain-Free Baked Nut and Fruit Granola. It contains no grains but instead nut flour, walnuts, almonds, dried cranberries, and other delicious ingredients. This is my favorite granola, and I could eat a whole twelve-ounce container in one sitting. I am keeping my fingers crossed that it can be merchandised and sold in sufficient volumes to succeed.

* * *

In 2013 Aurora decided to open a small retail outlet on Post Road, about a half mile from our factory. The sales from the store and the interactions with the public helped us gauge consumer interest in various items. The store offered Aurora's foodstuffs, specialty oils such as flavored olive oil and nut oils, and a variety of other gourmet items.

Another reason for setting up the store was personal; it satisfied my desire to open a small boutique food store that would carry Aurora's snacks. The store was named Wild Acorns and was managed by my husband Steve, who was semiretired.

In the store we got some suggestions. Our "roast your own almonds" idea came from using the Tuscan-flavored oil that was so popular at the store. I told Steve to keep his eyes and ears open for new suggestions. One idea was to sell, as part of the Aurora line, nut oils that were popular at the store. However, we decided not to carry them at Aurora due to competition. Also, oils were not sold in the produce section of stores where our product line is planogramed.

Other items for which Steve received several requests were acai, goji berries, and gooseberries. We tried them at Aurora, but they were slow sellers and eventually discontinued.

Some interesting comments made by consumers were relayed to me. One day Steve came home and told me he had a strange day. A man entered the store wearing a tight-fitting shirt with the first three buttons undone, showing off his chest hair, and wearing gold chains, bracelets, and a stud earring. His hair was slicked back, as he appeared to be intent on recapturing his youth. Steve was standing in the back of the store as Midlife Crisis Man called out loudly, asking if the store sold coconut oil. He went on to say, "My fiancée has a very sensitive vagina, and we've tried all sorts of creams, but they all irritate her skin. We went to the VIP [Very Intimate Pleasures] store, and they recommended coconut oil, which they don't carry. They suggested we try your store."

Steve offered him our selection of jar sizes of coconut oil to choose from. He also gave him a handout sheet on thirty popular uses for coconut oil. The customer's use was a thirty-first one that was not on the list. We chose to leave it off. To this day my husband and I chuckle at this unusual request.

* * *

Another time, Steve came home telling me he ordered a bottle of krill oil. Three customers had come into the store looking for it after seeing on *The Oprah Winfrey Show* how good the oil is for your health. I started to think that maybe Aurora could sell some nuts roasted in krill oil. That idea died immediately when I learned how expensive the oil was—over five hundred dollars a liter. In addition, krill oil has a very fishy smell that is not appetizing.

The saddest part of the story was when the three consumers came back to the store and Steve told them excitedly that he'd purchased the krill oil for them, they said, "Nah, it's too expensive. We were just curious if you carried it." Only one consumer bought a single two-ounce bottle of krill oil. We kept the oil for over three months, finally realizing we would have no buyers, and it would be getting rancid. The only options we had for getting rid of it were to find a baleen whale to buy it or to dispose of it. Since no whales shopped in our store, we tossed it.

Wild Acorns was a beautiful store but in a difficult location to park at and enter without crossing traffic. Steve actually had an accident in his car trying to cross the busy lane to get into our store's lot. Plus, there was a Whole Foods right across the street and a Trader Joe's next door. As they say, "Location, location, location."

Setting up the store and listening to Steve's interesting stories were unforgettable experiences though. Summing up my feelings is a paraphrasing of one of my favorite adages, "When I die, I'd rather be thinking of all the things I've done wrong or should have done differently than the things I wanted to do but didn't." I'm so glad I tried Wild Acorns, even though it failed, and I lost money on it.

> **You need to constantly keep your eyes and ears open to what's new in the market. Never stay stagnant.**

As I said before, when you own a snack-manufacturing company, you need to constantly keep your eyes and ears open to what's new in the market. Never stay stagnant. Over the years, we developed dozens of different granolas, trail mixes, glazed nuts, and flavored pretzels and plantains. Some succeed; most don't. But you can never give up. Like a shark, you must keep moving to survive.

In addition to developing new products, we always keep our eyes and ears open for new opportunities through acquisition or strategic partnerships. To date we have not found anything that has come to fruition, but opportunities are still out there.

\* \* \*

One company we delved into was a specialty bakery that sold cookies to gourmet sections of stores, brownies to airlines, and gourmet baked goods through the internet as corporate or personal gifts. My husband came with me as we drove to look at the facility of this company. After a lengthy presentation in the conference room, we took a tour of their plant. Most of the equipment was old, and we noticed production was a labor-intensive operation.

Sales were about eleven million dollars but with zero EBITDA. This means they were making no profit. We asked them what they wanted for a price, and after much skirting around, they said their figure was about nine million dollars. My first thought was *What are they drinking in their coffee cups, and can I have some?* They wanted nine million dollars for a company that had been losing money for the past few years?

"We have investors that need to be paid off," they explained. "If we don't find a buyer, we can get some more capital from others since we believe our company has a lot of untapped potential." Why would investors pour more money into a business that is losing money and has no particular niche or specialized equipment? Plus, why hadn't the "potential" been tapped?

We were prepared to offer about three million dollars because we thought we could leverage their baking products and customer base, particularly the airlines. But we declined the deal due to their adamancy about an outrageous price.

* * *

As mentioned earlier Aurora built a kitchen to make our own granola. A couple of years after our bakery was established, we received a few requests for gluten-free granola but could not bake it in our kitchen due to our use of wheat in some products. Coincidentally, about that same time, a woman approached us wanting to sell her small company that baked gluten-free granola. She had only two employees. I thought purchasing her small facility might be an excellent opportunity for us to offer gluten-free items.

When visiting her facility, I realized it was only two rooms. She mixed her gluten-free granola in a plastic barrel used for mixing mulch. The next room contained ingredients for another product that was not certified gluten-free. In essence she was not gluten-free because the rooms and equipment were comingled. Like us when we started as a new company, her operation was so small that it fell under the radar for the FDA and health department to investigate. We passed on purchasing the company. Finding no buyers for her business, she eventually closed and came looking to us for a job.

We investigated other small companies such as manufacturers of dried kale and baby foods and a company that roasted gourmet nuts. The company with gourmet nuts was the most interesting. But although they were a recognized brand and had a good reputation, they were too expensive.

Another company worth mentioning was a company much larger than Aurora but with a poor reputation. Again, people who work in the commodity market are a close-knit community. If you renege on a contract or negotiate unfairly, your name will be recognized—and not in a good light. I didn't want anything to do with this company or its reputation.

* * *

One interesting tale is of a young woman who came to my office looking for advice. She was tall, in her late twenties, and well spoken. She had made an appointment to see me and to share some thoughts on starting her business in making granola. The young woman was doing her homework. She had gone to several stores to see if they had any interest in her product.

One small chain, Morton Sloan's Associated Stores in New York, sent her to me for advice. Morty, the owner, liked to help women develop their businesses and was one of my first customers. This woman came into my office with a small clear bag of her granola, baked at a commercial kitchen in a local gourmet market. We went over all the facets of developing her brand, from nutritional values and allergens to delivery and packaging.

Eventually this young woman went into partnership with a colleague who excelled in marketing. Between the two of them, they were able to bring their business to tens of millions in sales in five years and eventually sold the company to Kellogg. In their start-up process, they decided not to make the granola themselves but instead to focus on marketing and developing a brand identity. They had copackers bake and package their granola while spending most of their funds promoting the brand Bear Naked. Eventually they built a facility to bake their granola.

I recall talking to this woman's partner, a young man, after they sold the business. I asked him if he planned to go to Harvard for his MBA now, considering that he'd gone into the granola business right after college. I was half-kidding, but he took the bait and replied, "Why go to business school to learn how to run a business when I just started a business and sold it for tens of millions of dollars? I should be teaching them." I couldn't argue with him.

Part of me was envious of this young couple for developing an outstanding company in such a short time and selling it for such a large sum of money. Yet I prefer to hold on to my company and continue running it—for the passion and fun of working with others. My goal is not just to make money but also to leave behind a legacy and a company that helps the community thrive. I have gotten numerous inquiries into investing in my business over the past ten years, but that just doesn't interest me at this time. I am concerned Aurora will lose its passion, direction, and sense of community if I bring in investors. I love this company and doubt if anybody can do a better job of running and growing Aurora at this time than the present group of employees and me. We are a team.

* * *

Many times I have been asked who my most significant competitors are. I could mention several companies that manufacture and sell snacks in my category, yet few of them sell all-natural and organic nuts, trail mixes, fruits, granolas, and beans of our quality. I don't want to bring up any competitors' names or make any comparisons of our brand to theirs except to mention one major competitor, Private Label.

When Stop & Shop was selling our line, they helped establish our brand by promoting it on the shelf and in shippers (those freestanding, corrugated display cases that are set up in stores). When they asked us to convert to their banner, it was a disappointment for us all at Aurora. When a supermarket chain decides that a line sells well and wants to put their label on it, the manufacturer will usually comply but will almost always prefer to keep it under their own brand. It's a lot more work producing a private-labeled brand for reasons previously mentioned. But more than this, brand identity is crucial. It is the recognition of the quality and consistency of a product. We've worked very hard on our brand, and it is a constant battle to discourage stores from wanting to purchase our brand and segue it into their own.

Working with commodities makes it that much more challenging to say no to private labeling. Nuts are nuts, and if you don't agree to private-label, the supermarket can go someplace else. However, if you have a value-added item with a reputation, you *can* say no. One such item for us is our granola. It is one of the top sellers in several stores, especially the Vanilla Crunch varieties. One chain showed great success with the granola, and after much negotiation, we agreed to cobrand the granola with their store's logo. But we are typically reluctant to compromise when it comes to our flagship products.

# THE UNION
# COMES A-KNOCKIN'

*The laboring people should unite and should protect*
*themselves against all idlers. You can divide mankind into*
*two classes: the laborers and the idlers, the supporters and*
*the supported, the honest and the dishonest. Every man is*
*dishonest who lives upon the unpaid labor of others, no matter*
*if he occupies a throne. All laborers should be brothers.*

—ROBERT GREEN INGERSOLL

The year after we made our final move to Orange, Connecticut—2014—the summer was a hot one. The new location was about a half-hour drive from Bridgeport, the city where most of our unskilled employees lived when we were located in Stratford. We'd been in business now for sixteen years and were still growing fast. Now that we had moved to Orange, New Haven became the closest city. Over 40 percent of our warehouse employees were new and came from New Haven since many of our previous employees had difficulty commuting from Bridgeport and needed to be replaced.

Several times before moving to Orange, we'd had unions stand outside our gates, soliciting employees to join. They claimed to offer better pay, more benefits, more vacation days, and representation when issues arise. In those days the employees who worked with Aurora felt like a family and shooed them away.

This time, however, when the union came knocking, a perfect storm was brewing. The weather outside was over ninety-five degrees and felt like a furnace. It was over eighty-three degrees within the factory, and we were using fans as our defense. The building was new, and the air-conditioning was not yet functional. Roasters, heat tunnels, and the bakery were adding to the heat. The union stood outside the gates with water and lemonade for people to drink as they left work. They carried big signs with a picture of an inferno, promising worker representation.

"We can help you get better pay! Better benefits! More holidays!" Aurora also had several new people who were leaders and agitators for the union and were stirring up the employees. Interestingly most of these people were not at Aurora a year later.

We were so busy with the move, hiring new employees, and finalizing the setup of equipment that we didn't recognize the seriousness of the situation. Most of the production employees, being new, had no loyalties to us and got caught up in the momentum. Meetings were held behind the scenes at people's homes to persuade others to join. Older employees were adamantly against the union, but new ones thought the grass would be greener on the other side. It was a difficult time at Aurora, with several arguments and altercations breaking out between pro-union and anti-union employees. A vote was held, the union won, and the production workers became unionized.

Part of me was upset at no longer having control of my own company. I felt like I had let my employees down, even though we had been fair throughout the years, giving decent raises and benefits as the company grew and Aurora could afford it. We also gave special perks such as picnics, bonuses, and loans to those who needed help. Aurora helped many employees in financial emergencies, such as pending evictions, without expecting to be paid back. I was concerned that the employees had made a mistake.

\* \* \*

After negotiations the employees were allotted some more annual holidays, but the benefits remained almost the same since we already offered decent benefits. People got raises, but I believe they were close to what we would have given them without the union's help. Since then, we have had to contact the union a few times, telling them we needed to raise certain employees' wages *above* our agreement, which they gladly agreed to.

A union is great if people are not getting fair pay and benefits. However, a union's influence can be frustrating for an employee who works extra hard yet is not compensated more than others who put in less effort. The union stresses equal pay regardless of performance. In addition, employees need to pay union dues with each paycheck and an initial payment to join.

I feel our union has been fair to Aurora. They have helped Aurora become more organized in our paperwork and

> A union's influence can be frustrating for an employee who works extra hard yet is not compensated more than others who put in less effort.

procedures. Also, to be honest there have been instances where the union has saved an employee's job when human resources may have been a bit hasty in suspending or terminating them. But the union has also saved jobs for employees who should have been let go several times and somehow snuck back under the wire. This is aggravating for those employees who need to pick up the slack to cover for them. Many of our employees work very hard to support their families. When a fellow employee is an idler and does not carry his or her weight, others need to work that much harder for the same pay.

Periodically an employee will come into the office expressing concerns about the union and wishing to eliminate it. At these times we stay out of the conversation to avoid any appearance of interfering and any issues with the union, which may claim we were stirring things up. Plus, we know that if the union is eliminated, another one will come knocking on the door, and they may not be as fair as the one we have. We are content with the union and will let the employees deal with union issues. At this time, we have no choice, as we've just finished negotiations for another three years.

# A BIG STEP FORWARD

*Sometimes serendipity*
*is just a revealed opportunity.*

I n 2018 Whole Foods decided to improve consistency for its private-labeled 365 program nationwide. They told Aurora they no longer needed our service, which entailed supplying them with over eighty private-labeled items on a regional basis for the East Coast. They thanked us for our excellent work and our partnership but felt that they needed to eliminate many of their smaller vendors in an effort to expand their 365 brand nationally while keeping pricing low and quality high. We were all walking around like zombies, depressed at having lost such an important customer and such a long-standing relationship.

About a month later, to our delight, we received a phone call from the buyer at global Whole Foods, saying they were interested in selling our Aurora branded items. He liked our product and had gotten positive feedback on us from the various divisions. We would no longer be regional but rather national. Distribution would be through a national distributor, and we would be considered a premium brand.

I felt like I was on cloud nine. Half of me felt we were being rewarded for all the hard work and dedication we had given Whole Foods over the past ten-plus years. I always admired their quality and commitment to selling only all-natural items and felt honored at being selected for their national program. The other half felt just plain lucky that we were not eliminated from their planogram. We vowed we would work our hardest to make them happy and remain a top-brand manufacturer.

This transition with Whole Foods has been a big help in allowing Aurora's brand to be recognized nationwide. We were now able to leverage this national distribution opportunity to pursue other stores and chains from Connecticut to California. We owe a lot to Whole Foods, not only for helping us develop our code of standards but also for helping us in our growth and in the development of our brand. We now distribute to chains throughout the entire United States. I love going to California or Florida and seeing our products on the shelf. It gives us such pride. In the past two years, we have hired salespeople in several regions of the country to promote our product line and work to secure new customers.

> **We were now able to leverage this national distribution opportunity to pursue other stores and chains**.

# GROWTH AND DEVELOPMENT

*Great works continue not only by strength and knowledge but also by perseverance in learning more.*

In 2017 Matthew had worked for Aurora as vice president of operations for over ten years. He told me he needed to spread his wings a bit and set up his own business, manufacturing electric bicycles. Behind the words of our exchange, we both understood that he was having issues at home and dealing with other personal matters. I also understood that he needed to get some outside experience and to practice navigating some situations he could not encounter at our family business. In addition, from Aurora's perspective, it was time we hired someone who had more experience than Matthew did at the time. Matthew had been a huge help to us, but it was time for a change.

So the mutual decision was made for Matthew to leave Aurora and see what else was out there for him. It was a win-win situation.

* * *

We immediately started looking at candidates for director of operations. After we weeded through several applicants, two finalists stood out as sharp, knowledgeable, and experienced. In the third interview, Scott—the preferred candidate—chuckled at a couple of comments made around the conference table. Six of us were there, asking him relentless questions, yet he seemed relaxed and very sharp—and he had a great laugh. That won me over, the laugh. At Aurora you need to have a good sense of humor and to go with the flow. At our office there is always a cacophony of laughter, talking, and sharing—and a dog barking. We all work hard, but we laugh hard too. So Scott became our director of operations and was promoted to vice president of operations a year later. It was a good decision, and he has brought Aurora to new heights.

The first year Scott came on board, he brought better organization and new ideas to Aurora. As the second year came around, we decided to purchase a pasteurization system, a million-dollar undertaking. This system pasteurizes nuts to eliminate enteric bacteria that can make people ill. In the past we had contracted with a company in a neighboring state that would steam-pasteurize our product by puncturing the bags of nuts with probes and subjecting them to hot steam while under pressure. We were concerned that this could be affecting the nuts' taste, texture, and viability, so we opted to purchase a piece of equipment more aligned with our natural credo. It uses an organic, plant-based fluid that oxidizes the outside of the nut to sterilize the surface. Oxygen and water are its by-products.

Two motives incentivized us in purchasing our pasteurization system. The first and initial motive was to become more vertically integrated, allowing us more independence. Vertical integration occurs when we roast, pasteurize, bake, and package our products from start to finish.

The second motive evolved as we set up the equipment. The idea struck us. "Why not pasteurize nuts for other companies—or 'toll-pasteurize'?" Although the top-line revenue from tolling is not high, the bottom-line profit margin is more than double what we make in selling our packaged goods. We were already toll-roasting nuts on an oil roaster we had. Why not toll-pasteurize too? It would augment our income and help us segue into other avenues.

As soon as word got out in the trade that Aurora had a valid system for roasting and pasteurizing nuts, the business expanded. Our roaster was being used so much that we decided to purchase a second one that produces over eight thousand pounds of roasted nuts per eight-hour shift. Today our tolling business continues to grow significantly, and we are becoming well known in the industry.

Selling retail products to supermarkets is getting more and more difficult, with larger companies purchasing smaller manufacturers and offering monies to supermarkets as incentives to put their products on the shelf. For smaller manufacturers to survive and grow, they need to bend with the changes around them.

> **For smaller manufacturers to survive and grow, they need to bend with the changes around them.**

Who knows? Ten years from now, our main focus at Aurora could be in tolling and processing of nuts as well as in manufacturing value-added items, as opposed to packaging nuts and dried fruits for supermarkets.

* * *

In processing nuts we always have some shrinkage and waste. It's sad to see product go to waste in cases where a food handler mistakenly mixes almonds instead of cashews into a thousand pounds of trail mix

183

or slightly over-roasts some peanuts. What do you do with the food? One option is to give it to a food bank, but most of the time, they want it in packages. We donate a lot of food to the food bank, but we don't want to package a thousand pounds of trail mix. That's a lot of added cost for the labor, packaging, and cardboard. Another option is to give the product to local farmers, which we have done in the past.

The third option is to donate it to Stephanie's Deer and Animal Sanctuary, as it's known in the factory. If there is waste, the production team will pack it up in boxes and stick it in my car. When I get home, my husband empties the nuts and trail mixes onto the top of our stone wall at the back of the house. As he walks to the wall, carrying boxes, I often see him popping nuts into his mouth, enjoying the fresh product that unfortunately cannot be used at Aurora. The deer love our open backyard, which is over three acres. We also feed foxes, coyotes, turkeys, squirrels, chipmunks, and all kinds of birds. We have the fattest animals in the neighborhood.

# THE PANDEMIC
# HITS AURORA

*Out of your vulnerabilities will come your strength.*

— SIGMUND FREUD

In March 2020 the pandemic came to Aurora almost overnight. Everybody in the office was nervous that our employees would get COVID-19 and mass hysteria would set in. What would happen to the business? What if everybody left? What if we had to close? What if truckers refused to pick up? What if, what if, what if?

Across the street from our facility, a veterans healthcare center set up a COVID-19 testing center. Cars would be lined up outside the building. Nobody was permitted to get out of their vehicle. Instead, a technician or nurse would come to your car to give you the test and would send the results to your home or doctor.

As the pandemic led to the closure of restaurants, people swarmed the supermarkets to load up on food and paper goods. Toilet paper was not to be found in any store. I always wondered why people made toilet paper a top priority and even had tugs-of-war over it at stores.

Other items that were difficult to get were hand sanitizer and disinfectant. For our business this was a big concern. We spent countless hours looking for vendors that could supply us with enough sanitizer for our needs as a factory. Consumers were hoarding it, making it difficult for businesses, not to mention hospitals and healthcare organizations, to procure necessary supplies.

Eventually three employees did come down with the virus, all in one day, and more than thirty production employees panicked and left work immediately. Since our facility is sanitized daily by our third shift, there is no need for additional scrubbing, for paying an outside firm to sanitize, or for us to close down. We were deemed as an essential business and were therefore allowed to stay open, providing we used all safety precautions possible.

Hours were reduced to enable the separation of shifts without overlap. At first, employees were upset at the cutback in their hours, but they came to understand the need for separation as the virus continued its path. Lunches were staggered, and employees needed to wear masks except while eating. We set up sanitation stations at all doors and followed the rules set by the government and Centers for Disease Control and Prevention (CDC) by giving employees paid time off for sickness or childcare.

\* \* \*

The higher demand for products at supermarkets resulted in Aurora's sales *increasing*. It was becoming harder for us to pack and ship, however, since people were not interested in working for minimum wage when getting subsidized to stay home. Plus, why expose yourself to COVID-19 if not necessary? We tried to entice our employees to continue working by offering them bonuses. Human resources was constantly on the phone, bringing in more people to handle the unexpected increase in volume and cover for those employees who needed to stay home for childcare. This was when everybody had to roll up their sleeves and help.

Several employees, including two of our salespeople, put on white sanitation hats and aprons and went to pack product on the production floor. Office employees who could not work in the warehouse were kept employed. Nobody lost their job. Some office personnel, after working for hours on the production lines, stayed late in the office or took work home with them to finish up. It was a busy time, but we needed to ensure orders were met and stores had their inventory. After a few months, we calculated our fill rate to stores and warehouses, and it was 99 percent. This was quite an accomplishment for any food business, considering supermarket shelves were half empty at the time. There were a lot of shortages as people hoarded.

A month or two after the breakout of COVID-19 in Connecticut, I received an unexpected email from one of my office employees. It brought tears to my eyes and made me so grateful for being in a position where I can affect the lives of others. It read, "Just wanted to send you a brief note to say that myself and many Aurora employees are thankful for everything you are doing to keep us safe and working. Leadership is unlocking people's potential to become better. Your leadership and dedication during this time have helped us grow into a better version of ourselves over the past few weeks. We've grown and adapted in ways most of us would have never imagined. Everyone can rise above their circumstances and achieve success if they are dedicated and passionate about what they do,

> **Everyone can rise above their circumstances and achieve success if they are dedicated and passionate about what they do.**

and you're our living proof of that." I rarely get letters of appreciation, so this one is a keeper.

* * *

As the vaccine was being introduced and COVID-19 cases started to decrease, we hoped things would revert to normal, except we wanted sales to remain up. But we were confronted by other obstacles, such as delivery issues, freight delays, and escalating costs. Truckers were in constant demand and raised their prices. Part of their shortage was due to COVID-19. Many truckers did not want to travel, much less make deliveries, across state lines. In addition, fuel costs went up, as did global shipping costs.

A trucker would often promise a delivery date, only to call back later, saying they could not pick the product up from its source. Despite their explanations we often knew it was because they got a better rate for somebody else's load. I know we are not the only company experiencing freight cost increases, but raising our prices to our customers during a pandemic is difficult.

In addition to higher freight costs, labor costs for unskilled laborers in Connecticut have increased, partially due to the pandemic. The minimum salary has been set for fifteen dollars per hour within the next three years, which will result in an increase of one dollar per hour per employee. That is a lot of money for a small business to absorb.

Costs of commodities and packaging are also rapidly going up, making it difficult for us to keep our pricing stable to our customers. Plastic alone has gone up 20 percent this year. We sell over one hundred and fifty commodities, and all but two have gone up or stayed the same this year. Usually, based on the crop year, some items increase in price, and others go down due to a good yield. Everybody is taking price increases.

COVID-19 continues to linger, and people struggle with questions about whether to get vaccinated, wear a mask, go out and socialize, etc. Yet Aurora continues to move forward, keeping our employees as safe as possible and doing our best to cope.

# WHERE WE GO FROM HERE

*You have brains in your head. You have feet in your shoes.*
*You can steer yourself in any direction you choose.*

— DR. SEUSS

Here I am in my late sixties, and I have so much more to do. Passion has been the driver of my journey and is what landed me at Aurora. Passion creates energy and leads to commitment. Nobody can ever limit my goals. Aurora, my family, and my friends have all been gifts in helping me fulfill my dreams.

As my mother used to tell me almost every day when she was in her nineties, "Life is so short. Where did

> **Passion creates energy and leads to commitment.**

all the time go to?" When I'm in my nineties, which is getting closer every day, I want to feel like I have taken a big bite out of life and lived it to the fullest. I don't want to be sorry for not trying certain things and feeling that I should have done this or that. I will never forget my Uncle Jack's words as he was suffering his last days due to an illness: "Life has been such a great ride. I wish I could go for another spin." At first, I felt sad for him but later understood he was recognizing the fun he'd had on his roller-coaster ride throughout life. He was a blessed man and knew it.

Aurora is still in its growing stages. We are presently working with a firm to add twenty to thirty-five thousand square feet to our existing plant because, once again, we are running out of room. We also purchased another roaster. In an ongoing effort to become less labor intensive, we are looking into buying some more automated fillers.

Tolling for other food providers has grown significantly, and we need more equipment. This new avenue of growth takes up a lot of space in our facility, and we hope it will bring in additional revenue and networking opportunities. Our next project involves offering updated packaging for nuts and trail mixes for supermarket chains. Larger-volume containers for families seem to be the trend. We hope we'll be lucky with this new introduction.

This book is not about a huge company but rather a small family-run business. Someday Aurora may grow into a company to be reckoned with. Yet no matter how much we grow, I hope we will continue to be family run and full of good people who care about Aurora. My kids grew up while I was developing this company, and they spent many hours either playing or working in various jobs within the production area or in the office. When they grew up, they helped the company mature into what it is today.

If the time comes when Aurora needs to be sold, I intend to be like Dr. Ericsson from the sex selection clinic Dick and I wanted to purchase. I will limit my buyers to only those who have the passion and mission for Aurora that I have. I don't want just an investor but rather someone who cares about what we do and takes care of my "child creation." Aurora was, and is, my dream. It's been a roller-coaster ride, and I don't want to get off for quite a while. It's too much fun.

Although I am healthy and could live well into my nineties like my mother, I doubt my brain will be as astute as it is now. So while I still have my brains and my feet, I will continue to steer my life, as well as the lives of those around me at Aurora, in a direction that is fun, nurturing, and a joy to pursue. There are still more sheltie puppies out there waiting to be mascots. Life is good, and I am lucky to have found a passion in life that has not only made me happy but has also given direction, employment, and purpose to others.

# PICTURES
# OF AURORA

*Stephanie with her dogs*

# ABOUT THE AUTHOR

S tephanie Blackwell lives in Fairfield, Connecticut, with her husband, two shelties, and the abundant wildlife in her backyard. Her interests lie in her family and her business, where she revels in the laughter and camaraderie of those around her.

*It is not about the length*
*of life but the depth of life.*

**—RALPH WALDO EMERSON**

Printed in the USA
CPSIA information can be obtained
at www.ICGtesting.com
JSHW012028140824
68134JS00033B/2943